A MORE DARING LIFE

Finding Voice at the Crossroads of Change

DAVID BERRY

PRAISE FOR *A MORE DARING LIFE*

"I have personally had the opportunity to know and work with David Berry for the better part of the past decade. His commitment to continuous improvement has been an inspiration to all of those who have had the opportunity to spend time with him. 'A More Daring Life' not only captures David's passion to help others achieve, but also provides invaluable insights into leading change, challenging convention, and moving toward the unknown. This book is representative of practical experiences, driven by a depth of knowledge, and paves the way to new thinking for driven leaders who aspire to make a difference in today's dynamic world."

—*David Abeles, CEO – TaylorMade-adidas Golf Co.*

"David's prescription for leadership is as simple as it is life-altering: To lead others, one must lead oneself. This choice isn't the easy choice, by far — it is far easier to write management memos and call meetings and cajole people into doing work and complain when they don't do it correctly. But it is far harder to look within, examine what is unexamined, and dare oneself to improve. Through sections on understanding, connection, and exploration, David shares his own search for voice, and creates a map for others daring enough to do the same. Highly recommended."

—*Jeff Shuck, CEO – Plenty Consulting*

"I know from a valuable consulting experience that David's ability to articulate concepts and give them life with a variety of different managers is admirable. It is no surprise that he has accomplished the same in written word. His analogy of the heart, the head and the voice is apt for the challenge of leading and getting the most from a work force. David first put his ideas and concepts to successful practice before sharing his insights in the form of this book. He is credible and he has a powerful message on leadership. He is a mentor and friend and now an accomplished author. I applaud 'A More Daring Life.'"

—Kirk Fowkes, Vice President - Hawthorne Machinery Co., a Caterpillar Inc. Dealer

"By bravely voicing his own stories – both the confidence-building victories and the humility-building foibles – David Berry gives us the empathetic but firm push we all need to convince us that it's time. It's time to let that inner voice be exposed so that we can become not just better leaders but more human as a result."

—Laura Garrett, SVP Human Resources – TaylorMade-adidas Golf Co.

"David Berry possesses the unique ability to pull from life stories and experiences the big ideas and concepts that help leaders transform organizations into places of collaboration, fulfillment and innovation."

—Allen Carlisle, CEO – Padre Dam Municipal Water District

For Theresa, my beautiful wife.

& For our children –
Duncan, Avery & Davis.

DEDICATIONS

STORYTELLER *is dedicated to the Invitas class of 2014/15.*

TEAM SPIRIT *is dedicated to the memory of Paul Salamunovich.*

CONNECTION *is dedicated to Duncan Berry.*

LINEAGE *is dedicated to Jeff Shuck.*

MAKING IT UP AS YOU GO *is dedicated to Marlene Laping.*

THE SPACE BETWEEN *is dedicated to the memory of Marion Smith.*

They want a wilderness with a map
but how about errors that give a new start?
or leaves that are edging into the light?
or the many places a road can't find?

Maybe there's a land where you have to sing
to explain anything: you blow a little whistle
just right and the next tree you meet is itself.
(And many a tree is not there yet.)

Things come toward you when you walk.
You go along singing a song that says
where you are going becomes its own
because you start. You blow a little whistle—

And a world begins under the map.

—William Stafford, "A Course in Creative Writing"

CONTENTS

PART II: *The Voice of Connection*

CONTENTS

PART III: *The Voice of Exploration*

ARE WE NOT SAFER LEADING A MORE DARING LIFE?

- Author unknown

PREFACE

On May 15, 2007, I published my first blog post. By "published" I mean that I copied and pasted Mary Oliver's poem, "The Journey," and sent it out under the banner of my new publication. Her remarkable poem is about making the choice to live the life you are meant to live. She conveys a frightening scene full of the dangers awaiting anyone who is willing to move in the direction of his or her greater purpose. A few short lines later she describes the promise of taking on such an adventure, the possibility of achieving nothing less than saving your very life. It is the poetic equivalent of the quote above.

By sending out this poem, I declared to the world my intention to be on such a journey. Brimming with nearly 20 years of pent-up Dead Poets Society-inspired enthusiasm, I proclaimed (à la Walt Whitman) that, "Yes! The powerful play does indeed go on, and I WILL contribute a verse!" It was time, finally time, to save my life.

"The Journey" would stand as my first and only post for the next 22 months.

I wasn't ready to make that contribution, after all.

My well-intentioned, but false, start was buckled under my belief that everything I had to offer had already been said and done (and far better than I could ever do it). I remember the fear of being labeled a hack and I allowed that fear to hold me back, allowed it to make me stay with the status quo and play small for nearly two more years.

I told myself that all I wanted was the courage to share my voice with the world. The truth, however, was that I was more interested in finding out if anyone would care. External validation had always mattered a little too much. And rejection? That was the worst possible outcome. Unwilling to endure even the potential for it, I did the only thing that made any sense: nothing.

Having stretched the idea of "baby steps" to a comical extreme, I was nearly 39 years old when I finally got moving. I had no choice because I was exhausted. All those years of waiting and wondering, of being "consumed by the grandiose ideas you have about your own importance," as Cheryl Strayed wrote in Tiny Beautiful Things (2012), had wrung me out. The only thing that made any sense, two years and a lifetime later, was to start again. In March 2009, I redesigned and rebooted my blog under the name "Specimen Life."

I took my inspiration from John Updike, who, in the Introduction to his memoirs said, "…my autobiography is my attempt to treat this life, this massive datum which happens to be mine, as a specimen life, representative in its odd uniqueness of all the oddly unique lives in the world…"

Someone commented that the name evoked images of the doctor's office and small plastic cups. I winced at that before realizing that it was precisely the point, because we've all had that experience. Updike taught me to embrace the universal in the particular. He inspired me to hold as true that my experiences – the more personal, the better – would connect and resonate with others because the language of our stories is universal. We have all felt afraid, alone, wanted, loved; we have all succeeded and failed. Since we all have our experiences of these feelings – and the stories that accompany them – we can easily find connections at the level of our common human experience.

I introduced the new blog as "a collection of experiences from my personal learning journey and my work inspiring that journey in others. My writing is a practice of expression, rooted in the knowledge that what is most personal is most universal."

I no longer publish under the banner, "Specimen Life," but I continue to write my blog, nearly 300 posts later. It is deeply gratifying to know that my intent today is no different than it was when I began in 2009. I continue to learn, and I want others to do so, also. I continue to express myself in writing because it both reveals and solidifies what I'm thinking and what I care about and helps me gather the courage to continue. And I know now, eight years later, that Updike was right in a way that was well beyond my capacity to understand or appreciate at the time: We are all "specimen lives." We are all "representative in (our) odd uniqueness of all the oddly unique lives in the world..."

Not long ago a friend asked me if I was thinking about writing a book. I told him that I was, but that I hadn't settled on my subject matter. The truth was that I was struggling with the process. "Well, why not just publish your blog?" came his next question. I had never considered it and his encouragement helped me to imagine the possibility of what I could do with what I had already written rather than continue to be frustrated with what I had not.

As simple as it sounds, it's taken me some time to get from that suggestion to this book. At first it struck me as a no-brainer. "Of course, just publish what I've got!" But then that voice in my head started in with criticisms like: "But that's not a 'real' book!" and "You're taking the easy way out." It was the same voice that I had allowed to hold me in check until I finally started writing and speaking about leadership and change in the public arena.

I didn't just want to publish a chronology of my blog: I wanted to share select pieces within a construct that would hold it together as a useful and meaningful resource for readers. I began to play with different models and approaches that would bring order to the chaos, looking to create a narrative out of many related but also disparate pieces. Finally, it occurred to me to organize the work around the ideas to which I pay most of my attention. These are the ideas that, when I have the humility and courage to practice them, make the most difference in the quality of my life and my leadership.

» *Understanding oneself*

» *Connecting with others*

» *Exploring and learning, always moving towards the unknown*

These practices are my guideposts, the tenets of a pragmatic philosophy for living and leading well in a world that is moving with an ever-increasing speed of complexity and change. When I embrace them, I can see and work with change as a natural, enlivening part of my experience. When I resist them, through my stubborn refusal to experience discomfort, complexity remains an enemy to be fought rather than a teacher to be honored.

Each of these organizing ideas is represented in the book's three sections or "voices." Each "voice" is introduced with a personal story as well as some additional context to both clarify and amplify its place within the larger work. In each case, what comes after is a collection of stories, insights and perspectives from my blog archive that demonstrate how I have worked with and been shaped by that idea over time.

The perspectives I express come from one of two specific points of view. First, I share the challenge of maintaining my commitment to a lifetime of learning. In these pieces I am usually talking about me. These are the selections that express my personal experience. They are reflections on the lessons and insights that reveal me to be just what I am, a "work in progress."

The second point of view is that of a consultant and a coach. In these pieces I am usually talking about you, and the organizations to which you belong. These are the selections in which I share my advocacy for and questions about the leadership practices I believe we need now. This advocacy has been shaped by my experience leading the coaching and leadership development initiatives at TaylorMade-adidas Golf Company and my work with executives and their organizations through my consultancy, RULE13 Learning.

This combination of expressions is my way of simultaneously practicing learning and leading. It is how I attempt to live out John F. Kennedy's admonition that they are "indispensable to one another."

You may not find each selection a perfect match for each section or "voice." In fact, many of them could fit well within another or even all of the other "voices." I'm okay with that, and I hope you are, too. My desire is that you find in these selections a source of support and inspiration for the expression of these "voices" in your personal practice of leadership.

Today, I spend my time working with leaders to build their capacity for resilience and purpose. I support them as they work to build organizations where people can find greater meaning and fulfill their aspirations. This collection is for them, because acting on these ideas is central to building organizations that can work that way. More broadly, this collection is for anyone – at any level – who wants to explore the relationship between self-understanding, powerful relationships, and the vital necessity for continuous learning and exploration.

Within each of us, right now, is everything we need in order to thrive – not survive, but thrive – in the face of complexity and change. We just have to decide whether or not we are willing to do the work, whether or not we are willing to lead a more daring life.

> **Words are the voice of the heart.**
>
> – Confucius

There are three reasons I chose the theme of "voice" to frame this call to lead a more daring life.

The first one is simple: I have extensive, first-hand experience with allowing my internal voice to shame my external voice into silence. And I know it's not just me. The list of people I have met who share this struggle is long, far too long when you consider how badly we need smart and thoughtful people to make their contribution.

Teacher John Keating, played by Robin Williams in the 1989 movie

Dead Poets Society, says it beautifully when he addresses a student who has refused to write a poem:

"Mr. Anderson thinks that everything inside of him is worthless and embarrassing. Isn't that right, Todd? Isn't that your worst fear? Well, I think you're wrong. I think you have something inside of you that is worth a great deal."

Secondly, the leaders we need today are those who are willing and able to speak up in the best possible way. I am referring to the ability to enter into and sustain the conversations necessary to creatively engage in a complicated world. This has nothing to do with increased volume or impressive eloquence. It has everything to do with the humility born of being in conversation with oneself and then extending that conversation to include and enable the wisdom of others.

The final reason for the theme of "voice" came to me one day as I was thinking about the often-challenging relationship I've had between my head and my heart, particularly my tendency to default to rationality and control when things get emotionally messy or uncertain. I recalled the desperation with which I had always tended to cling to my strategic mind when the vulnerability of an open heart would have been a more resourceful, if much more frightening, way to respond. The closer I looked at this pattern, the more clearly I saw just how far apart my head and heart could be, their close physical proximity in my body feeling more like miles and miles of rugged terrain.

More curious now, I decided to measure the physical space between them. I discovered that my head and my heart are a mere 18 inches apart! It was strangely gratifying to have that number, a tangible way to speak about a short, but difficult, distance. As I stood there looking in the mirror, tape measure still in hand, something else occurred to me. I noticed that my voice box seemed to sit right between them. I wondered if it was just the angle of my perspective but another quick measurement confirmed my suspicion. It's 9 inches from my forehead to my throat and 9 inches from the center of my chest to the same spot. Only 18 inches separate my head and my heart, and the place from which I speak the words each leads me to say is placed directly between them.

This symmetry makes perfect sense to me. Our physical design is intended, it seems, to be a model for the quality and nature of our expression. It's as if we are built with an equal capacity for rationality and vulnerability, for the known and unknown, for the measurable and immeasurable.

Our voice serves as a meeting place for both love and logic. We play, create and relate out loud. Though the expressions of head and heart can come through writing, touch, artistic creation, research, movement, and other nonverbal disciplines, they most often come into the world through the voice. That voice, when it speaks simultaneously and responsively from both head and heart, gives us the power to navigate change. Each domain is a distinct sensibility that, when paired with the other, helps us orient to the unknown. The strategic mind alone would likely default to the practices of the past and the comforts of the known. The heart alone would likely default to a kind of loving stasis, entranced by possibility but unable to determine which way to turn. With our voice being equidistant between our heads and our hearts, we are designed for integration, and yet we struggle so much to achieve it.

Why is that? If the voice is a meeting place for these two essential expressions, why is it that the head always seems to get there first? Why, for so many of us, are rationality and control so consistently our "go to" responses rather than feeling and vulnerability? Why do I so often have an impulse to open myself up only to be overwhelmed by the need to close down? Is it as simple as a defense against uncertainty? A paralyzing fear of the unknown? What makes us say "no" when the person next to us so desperately needs our "yes"? A belief that we will be somehow diminished if we give something away?

I can only speak from my own experience. I can only answer for myself. And to all of these questions my answer is this: my heart is a fragile thing, and I am committed to protecting it. I want to keep it safe. And I suspect that many others of you feel just the same way.

But that kind of safety is an old seduction. It promises something that it can't deliver. And for leaders – people who want to help others author stories of meaningful change – that kind of safety is the biggest limitation I can imagine.

We've got to give the heart at least an equal opportunity to be heard. We've got to help it guide the voice fully and in a timely manner, not just play second fiddle to the head. The head struggles to admit it, but it needs the heart to soften its edges, to temper its insistence on polarization and its compulsion to control. Each of the "voices" of this book, if they are to be spoken with full authority, is dependent on this happening. Here's why:

The Voice of Understanding strives for fluency in all of the ways that we are who we are: our values, purpose, strengths, limitations, and aspirations. It speaks to an accurate perspective on our past and present selves while holding an ongoing conversation about who we are becoming. Although we can rationally understand the influences of our past experiences and the ways they shape our present behaviors, it is only through feeling those experiences at the heart level that we can achieve a deeper comprehension of their impact. This voice creates the space, perhaps for the first time, for us to experience empathy with ourselves.

The Voice of Connection strives for fluency in all of the ways we pursue the reciprocal benefit of meaningful relationships. It speaks to our desire to be known and our opportunity to help others do the same. Although we can rationally understand the importance of relationships and appreciate the value of playing off of one another in the spirit of discovering what we have in common and the differences that make us complementary, it is altogether different to really experience – to feel –the chaos of collaboration, the depth and intricacy of individual needs being met through mutual commitment.

The Voice of Exploration strives for fluency in the language of possibility. It is the natural outcome of our commitment to Understanding and Connection, and it speaks to the necessity of exploration as the only response to the seduction of the status quo. Although we can rationally understand the necessity to venture out into the world to explore, learn, and discover, it is another thing altogether to actually feel our vulnerability in the face of the unknown. To enroll in the class, hold the violin and bow, walk onstage for the first time. To decide to adopt any new practice or behavior because our old ones no longer serve us or because we are simply ready to expand our capacity. We have to feel that energy in a place the mind doesn't dare to go – our heart.

These voices, taken together, are levers for activating the qualities of the heart. As we enhance them, developing our fluency, we enhance our capacity for leadership that can withstand the assault of complexity and change. As we develop them, we enliven the best qualities of our basic humanity, creating the conditions for others to do the same.

This is what I want for myself. This is what I want for those I love.

But I can only encourage you, implore you, to explore for yourself.

There is no certainty.

There is no safety.

There is only the opportunity to know ourselves better, to connect with others and work together to learn what the world has to teach us.

In the face of complexity and change, this is all we've got. It is also all we need.

PART I

THE VOICE OF UNDERSTANDING

THE FIRST PRODUCT OF SELF-KNOWLEDGE IS HUMILITY.

- Flannery O'Connor

INTRODUCTION

For just a moment, I considered staying in bed. It was 6:15 a.m. and my commitment to getting out for an early hike was being tested by the darkness of the hour. A peek out the window had me convinced it was the dead of night and the thrumming rain only strengthened my impulse to hunker down for a little more sleep.

I was in a cabin on the grounds of the Whidbey Institute in Washington State, a property crisscrossed by forest paths I had first seen in the light of day the previous afternoon. During that well-lit walk in the woods, I realized with satisfaction that the trails would provide an ideal way for me to get some exercise each morning of the leadership conference that I had traveled here to attend.

But once I'm up, I'm up. And I can be a stubborn guy when it comes to changing my plans. Dismissing the darkness, the rain, and my embarrassingly limited knowledge about the property, I got ready to go.

A trail map in one pocket and a small flashlight in hand, I headed down the lane with my usual confidence and a focus on completion. I might as well have taken along a candle and a fortune cookie, so closed-off was I to any form of help. With huge drops of water tumbling from the pine trees above and mud squishing under my heels, I was enthralled by the moment and blind to my arrogance.

I had concluded in reviewing the trail map that by navigating the intersecting trails in just the right way I could construct a three-mile loop that would maximize the uphill climbs. It was this loop I was seeking as I crashed into the darkness, assuming that what made sense on paper would materialize before my eyes. It did not, and I got lost. Again and again I was forced to stop, frustrated and breathless, so that I could reorient to the path. I did not complete the route I set out to do. I was lucky to get back in time for breakfast.

On the second morning, I was smarter but no wiser. I was not ready to do the essential thing required of walking in this unknown forest in the darkness: to slow down and notice. I would not let go of my head's agenda, still believing that I could just figure it out along the way. I backtracked multiple times, misread the map, and found myself at the end of a trail in an open field next to a school. It was one of many recalculations that only took me farther off course.

On the third day, in what I believed was my growing humility, I committed to a different approach. I took the flashlight along but left the trail map in my room. I reasoned that this would leave me no choice but to rely on presence. I would have to notice what was around and available to me at a given moment. I would have to slow down to see the trail markers and to recognize aspects of the landscape I had seen before and could use for guidance.

I got lost again.

This time, I was incredulous. Although I had good intentions, my actual choices did not back them up. I wanted to slow down, but I just wouldn't do it. I wouldn't let go of my head's need for completion and achievement. As I contemplated the perilously steep incline of my learning curve, I shuddered to think how a fourth encounter would have gone. My saving grace was the reality of scheduling and a return flight home.

I like to think I would have finally "discovered" the forest in the way that it was so patiently waiting for me to do. I like to think I would have taken care with my time and energy to assess and clarify the best path. Perhaps in a few days (weeks?) something would have shifted. Some new awareness born of the repetition of my obstinacy might have emerged, and little by little I might have started to learn. Perhaps.

I recognize that this kind of insistence – a stubborn refusal to accept the reality of my circumstances – says an awful lot about my particular makeup. I also know that I am not alone in this. What I see, as those who are most afflicted are best equipped to do, is a raft of leaders continuing to do things that no longer make sense. We are operating under radically different conditions than we are used to and we are ignoring the resources at our disposal. We are acting more like heroes on whose shoulders all responsibility must fall rather than like learners who are vigilant in their curiosity.

Doing the same thing, only faster, is an insufficient response to complexity and change. We have to make a different choice in the face of the unknown. We may, finally, just have to stop and get our bearings, about as radical a thing we can do in a world that is constantly on "go." Coming to a standstill has a way of getting our attention in a new way. What might happen if we stopped long enough and frequently enough to get a deeper understanding of ourselves? What might happen if we made just enough space for a new conversation about why we are so insistent on continuing down paths that no longer serve us?

In my experience, this courageous look within allows us to get a handle on who we are and why we are that way. It opens us up to what we care about and what we're afraid of, what we do exceedingly well and how we get triggered and stuck. Finally, it allows us to get clear about what it is we want from our personal and professional lives. In that inward-looking action, through the good, hard work of deepening our understanding, we gradually shape a new tone of voice. We equip ourselves to participate more fluently in the vital conversation about how we impact the people around us, our friends, family and those we lead.

When we start within – looking first at ourselves and at our biggest opportunities for growth and change – we admit to the truth that nothing else can shift until we do. We own the power of our leadership as a model, both good and bad, for others to follow. All of our choices and behaviors are declarations to those we lead about what we expect of them. "Do as I say, not as I do" is a sad refrain from another era. The question each of us has to decide is if we will choose to be more conscious and purposeful models for our colleagues or continue to allow our unrecognized and ineffective behaviors to set the tone? How will we change before asking others to change?

When we decide to discover who we are and determine to experience ourselves with the courageous vulnerability that such self-discovery requires, we create the conditions for others to do the same. We begin to normalize understanding oneself as the necessary prelude to the learning that takes place in our relationships and in our exploration of new possibilities. This ripple effect of self-awareness has the potential to transform our teams and our organizations, if only we are willing to get started.

The Voice of Understanding describes the ongoing experience of coming to terms with your deepest assumptions and beliefs about yourself. It is an opportunity to explore and define your values, to get clear on your purpose and vision, to honor your strengths and confront your limitations. It is the moment, perhaps for the first time in your life, to do an honest accounting of all that you are and all that you hope to be.

It comes down to this: your best chance for the successful exploration of the unknowns you face at the crossroads of change is through the exploration of the unknowns within yourself. For this, you must engage your Voice of Understanding.

The pieces I have included in this section were chosen to inspire your investigation. They are reflective of my own coming to terms with the patterns and behaviors of my life and the ways I have and continue to wrestle, embrace, and shift them in pursuit of becoming the person I want to be.

STORYTELLER

{May 8, 2015}

There is an end to every story. If we are to begin a new one,
how can it be otherwise?

In a small clearing in the woods I discover a pile of rocks and I imagine
that each is named for an old story I no longer need to know.

I picture myself tossing them into place, a mound forming as gray
stone thuds down upon gray stone, dusty paperbacks tumbling from a
cardboard box.

I have lugged them around long enough. They have been read and read
again, each turn of the page revealing familiar words and predictable plots,
faint notations marking futile efforts to mine new learning.

With a hint of loss I send them to the pile, recalling their past if limited
usefulness, and noting with both empathy and surprise just how small they
now seem. Immovable boulders reduced to toss-able rocks. Fragments of
former truth.

I carry a stone in my pocket. I selected it from a basket of gratitude and
blessing. Smooth and black, its rounded edges tell the story of elemental
shaping. There is a ridge running along half of one side, an invitational
crease, the line of disruption a reminder of possibility. It is my touchstone,
the shape of a new story. It comes with me now.

The others I have left behind.

I IMPLORE YOU,
I CHALLENGE YOU,
TO LIGHTEN UP,
GET DIRTY AND
TAKE SOME RISKS.

SELF INSPIRED

{March 29, 2009}

I wrote this "letter to myself" in October, 2005, as a participant in "Life Launch", a personal discovery and renewal workshop offered by the Hudson Institute of Coaching. I was there to fulfill a prerequisite for their coach certification program. Completing an assignment to write a letter from the 70-year-old version of myself, I composed what follows. It resonates to this day as the touchstone for my voice of understanding.

Dear David,

I've always believed in you and I've always known that the special combination of qualities, talents, skills and attributes that have come together to form your personality would sustain you in leading a vibrant, meaningful and exciting life.

Why did you stop taking risks? What are you so afraid of?

Where's the high school kid who talked his way into meeting Henry Kissinger and owned the stage? Where's the boldness – the sheer force of personality that changes the energy of a room, draws people to you, creates opportunity, and brings you joy? I challenge you to reclaim that. I challenge you to lead the second half of your life – starting now – to deliver what is most essentially you: strength of character, passion for aesthetic beauty and absolute belief that you can and should associate with the best and brightest minds of your generation.

Stop second-guessing yourself. Knock off this shit about measuring up, comparing, critiquing. Reclaim the 16-year-old and choose that you are going to apply all of that positive confidence and deliberate living in a new and more powerful way. Think about it: if you combine all that you've learned – all of your experience, reading and maturity – with the risk-taking, possibility-craving attitude of that young man, you will be an unstoppable, irresistible force.

Somewhere along the way you started to play it safe, to stay clean. You got too serious and you dampened the purity of you. I implore you, I challenge you, to lighten up, get dirty and take some risks – model a life lived in exultation and expectation.

I am proud of you.

I want to be inspired by you.

MORE ALONE =
MORE ALIVE

{January 27, 2010}

...the more I am willing to face–the more I am transformed...

I want to write about my aloneness. And, I want to write about my aliveness. I am uncomfortable with this marriage but their coexistence is both real and essential. I have learned through direct experience that the deeper I go into my development– the more I am willing to face – the more I am transformed; separated from the older versions of myself, stepping into a new inheritance, a new way of being in the world.

The problem is, this "stepping into" isn't at all a singular act or moment when what was unknown is now known. The transformation happens in complete darkness. Faith is required at the very moment when I have none. Dark is scary. Scary is intimidating. I want to go back.

Enter aliveness. It is the very fear of the dark, the aloneness, which is paired to me like a twin, reminding me that I am wholly alive. It is in the desperation of the feeling that the transformation is not occurring, that the evolution is not actually real, that I feel most aware of my own presence, my own inhabiting of the world. I never notice the air except when I cannot breathe.

I am engaged in a quiet war with my coercive self. It is telling me an old story about who and what I am, attempting to drown out the new self that is emerging. The enemy says that I fight alone, that there is no help for me. And, though I am rationally aware that help is all around me (the air I breathe, for starters), it is easier to succumb to the old story of abandonment.

The challenge to me is to see more. To see the help that is there. To live from my innocence and hold the belief that, though shrouded in darkness, the transformation is happening, is real, and must be midwifed into existence.

CAREFUL, CAREFREE, CARELESS

{March 15, 2010}

The closer we come to beating down the resistance, the more it tries to retain control.

Careful: controlled, exact, fitting-in, cautious, fearful, heavy, reliable, dependable, conservative, edited, unknown, uncertain, judgmental, closed

Carefree: light, refreshing, spontaneous, enjoyable, infectious, in-the-moment, willing, open, friendly, authentic, vulnerable, silly

Careless: reckless, wasteful, undependable, restless, loose, standing-out, sloppy, fearless, dangerous, risky

These are my words, my definitions, of three terms that are extremely important to me right now. I want you to notice how my definitions reflect my feelings about these words. Notice the judgment, the discomfort and the aspiration. For me, these are heavily loaded terms.

On the continuum of careful to careless, I've long made my home on the left-hand side. At the risk of oversimplifying the "why," it really comes down to childhood compensations that are really tough to let go of as an adult. As a 10-year-old kid whose family has been fractured, of course you're going to go for "controlled, fitting-in, cautious." I look at my 10-year-old son and what his "concerns" are and I'm convinced that kids that age aren't ready to take on that much "careful" without it having some long-term impact.

It's time for those old compensations to go. Not that it's that easy —I've been chipping away at them for years now. I think I'm just so damn close to reaching a new level of freedom that I feel the constriction as freshly as I ever have. Isn't that always the way? The closer we come to beating down the resistance, the more desperately it tries to retain control. I just see it for what is and I'm over it. The old control needs are massively limiting, holding me back from expressing myself, risking more and giving chase to my dreams.

I think my closest friends and family would say that I am "carefree" a lot of the time. A few have even borne witness to my "carelessness." That's about safety, the strength of relationship, the certainty of real trust and acceptance. All of which equates to a low-risk environment.

I'm in pursuit of that same level of "carefree" (with at least an occasional dash of "careless") when the risk is higher – new circumstances, new relationships, new environments – when most people are happy to just fit in. I don't want to just fit in; I do that on autopilot. I want to stand out, to be distinct, to be remarkable because I'm willing to express who I am, what I think and why with as much transparency, vulnerability and authenticity as I can muster.

MY DRAGON TAIL

{April 13, 2010}

I was not ready to trust myself because I viewed my life through the lens of comparison and deficit rather than the lens of acceptance and generosity.

Coach and author Doug Silsbee shares a metaphor that has immediate and powerful relevance in my life. Maybe it's because I just turned 40 or because I am beginning to own both my earned and inherited gifts, but the lesson of the dragon tail landed hard and well. Doug asked us to imagine that we each have a long and powerful tail in which reside our lineage, our experience, our competence, our learning and our achievements.

Attached to us as it is, residing in us as it does, it is with us all the time. If we are mindful of its presence, it swings behind us with assuredness, stabilizing us and allowing us to be more present, available and generous.

I spent so much of the last decade of my life looking for what I did not have, for what wasn't there, instead of capitalizing on what was available. I was not ready to trust myself because I viewed my life through the lens of comparison and deficit rather than the lens of acceptance and generosity.

Now that I feel that tail swinging behind me, I am shifting. I stand in front of a room, I sit across from a client, confident in what I have to offer but no longer tied to a vision of perfect or a vision of failure that is consuming and debilitating. There is freedom in the tail; recognition and trust that each new circumstance is an opportunity for all of me — lineage, experience, competence, learning, achievements — to show up and offer what I have to give.

THOUGH MY
LINEAGE MAY BE
UNCHANGEABLE ITS
FUTURE PROGRESSION
IS IN MY HANDS.

LINEAGE

{April 18, 2010}

A dear friend faced the gut-wrenching responsibility of eulogizing his father, tragically taken away too soon. With courage, passion and deepest respect he entered the moment, bringing with him a family history, a legacy he described this way: "a legacy that my grandmother called 'the red blood of the pioneers' –- a legacy born of centuries working the soil, the fortitude to keep walking forward in the face of the inertia of the world."

To know my friend is to know that this legacy is not about him, it is him. To know him is to understand, without ever hearing the words, that he is the pioneer, the present chapter of a long and fascinating story. The evidence of it– his work, values, motivations and adaptations – is so compelling, so true. He is living out the best of his lineage as he is opening up to the harder questions it also contains.

There is weight and power in both acknowledging and accepting my inheritance. How is it present in me today? In what ways might I strengthen and advance the storyline through my beliefs, commitments and actions?

I am the son of clergy, teachers and doctors; naval officers and farmers. I see in myself the impassioned preacher, both faithful and questioning. I see the confidence and the bedside manner if not the scientific aptitude. I see the respect for ritual and protocol, the keeper of traditions. I see a cultivator and a catalyst.

And while I am proud and honored to live out these attributes, they are only part of the story. I also have within me aspects of my inheritance that I feel responsible to change. Living in me are some hard truths about what came before that can either be confronted now or passed along to my children. Though my lineage may be unchangeable, its future progression is in my hands. As it continues I have a profound opportunity to influence the feel and focus of its forward path. By doing so, I honor those who came before by applying the lessons of the present to the patterns of the past.

THE FIRE FOREST

{August 15, 2010}

When we are caught in a pattern of our own making and it has outlived its usefulness ...we've got to create the fire forest in our own life.

The longleaf pine woodlands in Georgia is one of the most fire-dependent ecosystems in North America. According to The Natural History of the Fire Forest by R. Todd Engstrom, et al. (2001), "...these woodlands depend on frequent fire (every one to three years) to maintain their biological richness and ecosystem health today, as they have for tens of thousands of years."

For the system to survive and to thrive it has to burn, clearing out the old growth to make room for the new.

When we are stuck; when we are caught in a pattern of our own making and it has outlived its usefulness; when we know there is a bigger "more" waiting for us but we have no idea how to move toward it; when we are deathly afraid of taking the next, new step because it is just so foreign and we feel just so helpless; that's when we've got to create the "fire forest" in our own lives.

From my own experience, I can offer two things: (1) The burn of that fire, fueled by underbrush, pine straw and ancient, explosive kindling, is a long, hot burn. (2) That burn produces a healing, life-giving heat that nurtures new growth like a greenhouse nurtures a tender seedling.

Just like the fire forest, each of us is a system that needs renewal; one that is capable of adapting to the cycle of regeneration and growing more richly and more abundantly because of it. Unlike the fire forest, we get to choose if and when we will enter the cycle and just how much fuel we will bring with us when we do.

EACH SMALL CHANGE
IS AN ESSENTIAL
PART OF DEFINING A
POWERFUL PRESENCE
WHILE HINTING AT
THE INEVITABILITY
OF WHAT'S TO COME.

SMALL THINGS – A WINTER ESSAY

{February 7, 2012}

In the northern latitudes, winter is a time of cold, snowy retreat. It is a time to battle the elements and be subdued by them all at once. It is a time of forced accommodation to nature's declaration that it has wrapped up another cycle of starting, surging and retreating, and is now resigned to lie in preparatory wait for the conditions that will allow it to begin again. All the while the creatures of this environment, human and otherwise, must adapt to surroundings that limit both their mobility and access and require a focus on economy of effort and the prevention of exposure. There is nothing subtle about it.

The Southern California winter, on the other hand, offers a more nuanced physical presence. It does not arrive with a blast of cold or a blanket of snow. It comes to us hesitantly and with purpose. It is recognizable in its very measured and quiet advance. I have learned to mark the arrival and progression of our winter by the quality of the daylight. Tilted further from the sun as we are at this time of year, it arcs lower in the sky and even at the peak of day offers a more diffuse and forgiving light. It is a small move, one you know has been underway for some time but that seems to arrive all at once.

Visitors from those far-off latitudes rejoice in our perpetual "summer" just as we are settling in to appreciate the subtle and comforting shift in light and growth. Without time and presence, it is impossible to fully appreciate that this is a stage of slight changes, small shifts in the light and the landscape that tell the keen observer that we are progressing from one place to another. The artist Andy Goldsworthy writes that "real change is best understood by staying in one place." He appreciates that when we are visitors to a place we only have its present context, not the awareness of what preceded it. We've missed the gradual changes and the many hints that told us it was coming. His work invites us to observe where we are and to appreciate how it is linked to where we have just been and where we are going.

The winter landscape, northern or southern, obvious or subtle, represents a significant slowing down of the natural world. And, though we may be tempted to see this as stagnation, it most definitely is not. The interlude of winter often masks the fractional alterations and the underlying energy that are present both around and beneath us. In the winter landscape there is a buzz of conservation, restoration and deep rooting. If it is not the time to go up, beckoned by warm soil and sun, then surely it must be the time to go across and down, to strengthen what can be strengthened in preparation for what's to come. On the surface, very little changes. Below the surface, there is an intense "getting ready."

In this specific winter reflection, I find myself humbled by the realization that I have been neglectful of those fractional shifts in my own learning, preferring to obsess over the big change yet to be achieved rather than on the slight changes that pave the way forward. The idea of progression, of building part-by-part and bit-by-bit, remains a foreign landscape, a place of excuse and rationalization for those who "just don't have what it takes to put it all together." And, yet, in the harshness of this judgment is a dawning realization of what is present and vital: that all of my learning is in service of both a vibrant present and a promising future. It is a recognition that the minor shifts in my interior winter landscape are no different than those in the world outside my window. Each small change is an essential part of defining a powerful presence – winter, here and now– while hinting at the inevitability of what's to come.

GETTING READY – A SPRING ESSAY

{April 9, 2012}

The itch for change seems to sneak up on us all it once. You feel a little silly that you didn't notice it before and now that you do you realize you've got to deal with it.

A perfect spring storm rolled through town last week. It rained hard for an hour or so and then it started to clear, precisely at sunset, a play of light and shadow, clean air and a majestic double rainbow, fully formed and arcing high across the sky to the east. A meaningful rain in Southern California is a rare thing but one that has all of those elements at once is exceptional, inspiring deep appreciation that a waiting world is waking up to a new dawn of growth and vitality.

Spring is here and what it yields it does so with fits and starts, warm and cool air fighting for dominance with the victor never really in doubt. Here at the beginning of the season, what was dormant and quiet through the winter begins to change its conversation with the landscape. With childlike innocence it says, "Here I am" and "Wait 'til you see this" and little by little that bulb pushes up a stem that finally breaks the surface and stretches up to be known again.

If we trust that our lives play out in accord with nature's seasonal shifts and if we notice how we experience transitions that seem to align with changes in the natural world, we should not be surprised. We are, first and foremost, biological. That we would see in our own lives a reflection of what's happening outside the window makes sense if we are willing to honor our integral, if often unrecognized, connection to the cycles and systems of which we are a part.

To borrow the language of the Hudson Institute of Coaching, there are times when we "go for it," times when we are in "the doldrums," times for "cocooning" and times for "getting ready." I have long found these to be synonymous with the seasons: summer, fall, winter and spring, respectively. Though we can experience them "out of season," each is marked by unique qualities and each calls us to engage in a new kind of conversation and relationship with ourselves and the world around us.

Thinking more carefully about the qualities of "getting ready," I can't help but consider the other realities of the advent of spring: the outcome and output of all of that new growth is that the air teems with pollen and other airborne matter finally freed from winter's prison. Spring breezes start to blow and the stuff goes everywhere. If you suffer from hay fever or other spring allergies, this is a season less about new growth and possibility and more about the anticipation and realities of discomfort: red eyes, stuffy noses and plenty of itching and scratching. And so it is that whether we actually experience allergic reactions to the "stuff" of spring or just feel the restlessness and fever of a season of "getting ready" – whatever time of year it might be – it can be an unsettling and uncomfortable period for many of us.

My personal epiphany this spring is that not only have I become restless about a few things, but the itchiness I feel is a cumulative one, the kind that's been sneaking up on me for a long time. I have heard it called a "blinding flash of the obvious." You feel a little silly that you didn't notice it before and now that you do you realize you've got to deal with it.

First, and most benignly, my wife and I recognized that some parts of our home were starting to look a little worn. A few cracks in the walls had stretched and widened; that great paint job we did when we moved in had lost its luster; the kitchen faucet hasn't worked correctly for precisely… always, and on and on. Taking all this in one day, it finally struck me: it's been seven years since we moved into our house and the inevitable itchiness we'd been feeling had become more common than not. And, easily enough, patchers, painters and plumbers were summoned to the task. See a problem and fix it; a kind of convenient scratching.

It also happens that this year marks the seventh anniversary of my employment with the organization where I started as a "training manager" and have most recently been named a "vice president." That progression of job titles brings with it a realization that our key initiatives, once new, fresh and invigorating, have developed some cracks of their own. Clearly, some maintenance is needed and the itch I need to scratch is that of reenergizing myself through the redefinition, reinvention and reconfiguration of my work itself. Where are the patchers, painters, and plumbers now, I wonder?

I realize that if I stay with something long enough, it requires me to reassess and revise my relationship with it. And there's something deeply satisfying about being around that long. There is also something daunting about tackling the interactions, conversations and decisions necessary to reinvent and recreate; the realization that there is no outsourcing this job; the realization that I am the patcher, the painter and the plumber. A fresh coat of paint is one thing; taking on the reinvention of a system of which I am only one part – a marriage, a cultural initiative, a team – is something else altogether.

This spring, I am steeling myself for that work. It is an intense "getting ready."

UNFINISHED

{February 2, 2013}

Maybe my willingness to just get started, to trust that the right elements will emerge along the way, is how the most vital learning will emerge. Perhaps my job is to learn to love the question of what it might become.

This is Rita. Full name: Margarita Rae Berry. She is a one-year-old Golden Retriever mix of energy, love, affection and destruction. We "rescued" Rita from an online pet adoption site a couple of weeks ago and, through a tumultuous "interview" process, decided against all better judgment and common sense to welcome her into our family. Rita was originally found on the streets of Tijuana – she came to us as "Hannah" but we renamed her as an homage to her homeland – and had lived in a number of foster homes in the last year. She's a healthy and happy puppy, but given her upbringing so far and her "big kid" status, she's definitely rough around the edges.

Rita is, by any measure, unfinished. It is that part of her that has spoken to me so loudly and clearly these past two weeks. Training her has been an incredible experience in behavioral conditioning, responsiveness, stubbornness and progress. She has been patient with me, however, and I am learning.

In her willingness to discover and explore, in her pushing of limits, challenging of boundaries and often misplaced and aggressive giving of affection, she is trying to find her way to acceptance and love. Her greatest gift is her lack of self-doubt. She possesses no irrational fears, does not second-guess herself, and seems utterly lacking in inner turmoil about how the world will perceive her should she fail. As I mentioned, I am learning.

I launched a new website for the sharing of ideas and experiences a number of months ago, but I have been hesitant to announce it to the world because it doesn't yet measure up to my expectations of what a "great" blog or website should look like. I have been unable or perhaps unwilling to reconcile myself to the possibility that it is the unfinished quality of it that may make it the most useful. Maybe my willingness to just get started, to trust that the right elements will emerge along the way. is how the most vital learning will emerge. Perhaps my job is to learn to love the question of what it might become.

Like me and like Rita, the site is unfinished. So are you. So is the world. It is the unfinished parts in each of us that make us deeply aware of our own vulnerability and our own fears. They are also the parts that make it possible to be empathic toward others as we offer to them what we so hope they will offer us in return. It is that part I am counting on from each of you. It is that part you should expect of me.

As I start writing again I aspire to do so with a spirit of discovery and exploration; to push limits and to challenge boundaries.

In other words: just how Rita would do it.

WHO AM I BEING?

{February 3, 2013}

His humble and massively vulnerable awareness is that his
followers are always a perfect reflection of his energy, his
optimism and his belief.

Benjamin Zander, conductor of the Boston Philharmonic, asks an
extraordinary question of himself when he does not see his players fully
engaged...when he does not see them "awake with possibility."

He asks, "Who am I being?" not, "Why don't they get it?" or, "What's
their problem?" He turns the question first on himself: "Who am I being
that I am not seeing the effort, the passion and the possibility that I know
is in every one of them?"

His humble and massively vulnerable awareness is that his followers are
always a perfect reflection of his energy, his optimism and his belief.

Is there an organization today that isn't facing the need to transform in
the face of a radically changing world? I would bet on those whose leaders
start the conversation with this profound and simple question:

"Who am I being?"

THE ONLY PERSON
WHO CAN SOLVE
THE LABYRINTH OF
YOURSELF IS YOU.

EVERY GOOD BOY DOES FINE

{April 19, 2013}

"There's a labyrinth of voices inside your head, a counterpoint of self-awareness and the remembered sayings of your guides and mentors, who don't always agree. Sometimes you wish you could go back and ask your teachers again to guide you; but up there onstage, exactly where they always wanted you to be, you must simply find your way. They have given all the help they can; the only person who can solve the labyrinth of yourself is you."

– Jeremy Denk

Precisely seven weeks ago today was the first day of the next chapter of my professional life. I declared, both in word and deed, to myself, my family and all who would listen, that I was stepping into new territory. I was pulled forward by the energy and possibility of the unknown, accelerated by my own evolving awareness of the limited window of opportunity to make the impact I want to make in the way I want to make it.

Sitting here in my newly fashioned home office looking out on a brilliant spring afternoon, I reflect with gratitude on my guides and mentors and how they have influenced me to get to this place. I am on my own path to mastery because of them and the most important lesson they taught me: that until I learned to look within, to go below the surface of myself and wrestle with and reconcile myself to what I found there, I would continue to grant authority over my life to others rather than claiming it for myself.

I freely admit that there are days when I don't want the freedom I have earned; that there is great temptation to bask in the guidance of those I have looked up to for so long, the underlying suspicion that if I hold those relationships where they are for just a little longer, I'll eke out just a little more wisdom and confidence for the path ahead.

But that's an old voice tempting me back to the safety of the known. And I recognize that it's much softer now. And getting softer every day.

This boy will be fine.

HOW TO BE INVISIBLE

{May 8, 2013}

I wasn't aware of just how much the sloughing off of an old skin can leave you unrecognizable to yourself.

There's a lot to learn when you're in transition. If you're like me, you don't want to spend too much time actually learning it though, because well, you know, you're in transition. And that alone is plenty awkward on most days. I find that taking the stance of a dispassionate, objective observer of my own experience during this time is particularly difficult. There are moments of insight, however, and this is one of them:

I'm learning what it feels like to become invisible. Not in a superhero kind of way. It feels a little naive to say that I didn't expect to disappear, at least a little bit, after making this change, but I guess I wasn't aware of just how much the sloughing off of an old skin can leave you unrecognizable to yourself.

I know this feeling of disappearance isn't a permanent condition, but if I wanted it to be, here's how I would go about it:

1. Be someone else's brand. I was walking through the airport the other day when I realized with some embarrassment that nearly everything I was wearing and holding – luggage, briefcase, shoes and attire – was branded by my former employer. It took me a lot of years to acquire all of that stuff and there's no good reason to get rid of it. What once felt like loyalty and commitment now just feels awkward and obsessive. Here were the vestiges of an old life coming together to remind me how penetrating that life was and how much it is no longer. I suppose our identities are a bigger product of our affiliations than I care to admit.

2. Spend more time listening to other voices than you do to your own. Through the generosity of friendship many people have offered me help in the form of insight, ideas and perspective. It's humbling. And, it's useful. It's also a place to get lost. To lose my own voice. It reminds me a bit of the title of Truman Capote's book, Other Voices, Other Rooms. There's always another voice in another room available to "talk it over" and "hash it out" and "think it through." There's a point at which this becomes a seductive exercise that feels productive and creative but can become a holding pattern, a clever form of procrastination. "Maybe this next conversation will be the one that breaks the logjam of ideas and possibilities?" Probably not. Because at some point you just have to sit down and do the work. (See The War of Art by Steven Pressfield).

3. Give in to your vices. Let's face it, transition brings up all kinds of vulnerability and uncertainty. It's exactly the time to comfort ourselves with, well, comfort. Another drink, a little more dessert, another movie, another show, sleeping late. None of this is bad stuff. It's just bad stuff when it becomes the rule instead of the exception. Transition is useful as a time to form new disciplines of physical and emotional renewal. It's just a hell of a time to get them in place and make them stick. It's so easy to think that "with all this free time I'll be able to do all this great stuff I've been wanting to do," like reading, meditating, exercise, etc. In my experience, it's much, much easier to do that when bound by the parameters of a working day forcing the creative use of time and energy.

4. Be hard on yourself. Beat yourself up for your need to maintain a connection to your old company, that old brand, because it reminds you of your contribution and your value. Criticize yourself for your need to talk to everyone you know to seek input, understanding and ideas about what's next because doing so deepens your own thinking and opens you to new insights. Allow the voices of guilt to be the loudest when you indulge your desire for a little more of the good stuff, relaxing into the truth that you do have this day in which to be however you want and need to be.

In transition, something old has to give way to the something new that is trying to emerge. We can try to rush the process, but experience tells me that doing so only accentuates the discomfort of transformation. Seeing ourselves anew requires that we tolerate the discomfort of the phases of change while holding on for dear life to whatever small vision we have of what we may become. It also requires that we forgive ourselves for the very human feelings and very real needs that accompany us as we turn our attention to a new way of being.

Jean-Léon Gérôme (1824-1904). Pygmalion and
Galatea (ca. 1890). Oil on canvas. 88.9 x 68.6 cm.
The Metropolitan Museum of Art/Art Resource, NY.

ORIGINAL

{September 23, 2013}

When you are original to yourself, you will find your own ground on which to stand.

In the Victoria and Albert Museum in London, there are two large halls called the Cast Courts. These galleries house plaster reproductions of some of the most famous sculptures in the world, many of them wearing better than the originals, given their protection from the elements. I haven't been to Florence but I have been able to experience Michelangelo's David thanks to this display. Strangely, these rooms feel more like warehouses than galleries, given that what they contain, impressively rendered though they may be, are only copies. They are crowded spaces with the likenesses of famous sculptures lined up row after row. The Courts are at once exhilarating and disconcerting, reminding me of the closing scene in Raiders of the Lost Ark when the Ark of the Covenant is unceremoniously crated up and placed into an enormous government depository.

I am mindful of this: if you settle for being a copy, you can still look impressive, but you will be lost in the crowd, your plaster preventing you from doing anything other than staying in a protected space. When you are original to yourself, your contribution to the world carved out of your very best marble, you will find your own ground on which to stand. Yes, you will be beaten up by time and exposure as you must surely be, but that is how you will know, once and for all, that you're not faking it anymore.

That is how you will know, like Pygmalion's statue, Galatea, that you have finally come to life.

WHAT FREEDOM
BEGINS TO MEAN
IS OUR ABILITY TO
REDUCE THE NUMBER
OF OUTSIDE AGENCIES
WE BRING TO BEAR
IN HELPING US NUMB
THE PARTS OF OUR
EXISTENCE WE JUST
DON'T WANT TO FACE
OR FEEL.

START WITHIN

{September 30, 2013}

Great leaders start within. They know who they are and why they are and they use that knowledge to manage their impact and effectiveness on those they lead. They have gone below the surface of their own experience, discovered their personal set of unpleasant unknowns, faced them, wrestled them and worked with them until they are no longer blindly held captive by them. They have done the internal work necessary to come to a penetrating understanding that everyone is fighting the same battle against the arrayed forces of unpleasant unknowns. This process makes them more human than otherwise and, as such, more thoughtful about the universality of the human condition. (Which means that if you are following them they are far more likely to be tuned into who you are, what you need and how to help you get it.)

What I must underline, though, is that what I am describing is a process, not an event. It is also never-ending. I know of no one who has undertaken the courageous act of honest self-reflection and awareness who does not have to work on it with continual and consistent dedication. It's damn hard work. However, once you find the freedom and peace that come with acknowledging and dealing with your own stuff, well, you will simply never go back.

What freedom begins to mean is our ability to reduce the number of outside agencies we bring to bear in helping us numb the parts of our existence we just don't want to face or feel. It means that we can start to be with ourselves, just as we are, when before we would use anything and anybody to prevent us from having to do so.

The comedian Louis CK, during an appearance on Conan O'Brien's late-night talk show, gave a beautifully honest explanation of why he wouldn't allow his kids to have smartphones. The brilliance of his observation is that it addresses our deep fear of being alone and sad and that, through the easy distraction of our smartphones, we are robbing ourselves of the opportunity to learn how to live and work with those essential human feelings. He said,

> *You need to build an ability to just be yourself and not be doing something. That's what the phones are taking away...is the ability to just sit there. Like this. That's being a person."*

The world is moving toward meaning. I am convinced of it. I am also convinced that the people who will lead the way are those with the most practice at 'being a person' as honestly and courageously as possible. Will you be among them?

STOP

{October 14, 2013}

I've come to the conclusion that the first and best thing to say
to anyone – especially those in leadership roles – about how to
be more effective is to simply 'stop'.

Take a deep breath.

Wherever you are right now, just pause for a moment and take a deep,
expansive breath.

Breathe in through your nose, expanding your lungs and pushing the
air all the way down to the bottom of your diaphragm.

Exhale through your mouth, letting all of the air escape. Now that
you've done it once, take a moment to take two or three more good deep
breaths and feel the difference it makes in your presence, your clarity and
your perspective.

To breathe this way you have to focus on it. You have to adjust your
posture to fully inhale and you have to become present to what you are
doing in a way that you normally don't, especially with something like
breathing. It's really worth it.

But this is not a post about breathing. This is a post about stopping.

I've come to the conclusion that the first and best thing to say to anyone – especially those in leadership roles – about how to be more effective
is to simply "stop."

The benefits of a meaningful timeout, whether it be for a few moments
of quality breathing, an hour of reflection and daydreaming, a brief walk
around the building, or a restorative weekend away, are both significant
and rarely realized. And we're paying for it. We have fallen victim to a

world of our own creation, constructed to demand our attention and feed our anxieties about missing out and falling behind.

When we stop, even briefly, we create space. In new space is the opportunity for new insights. New insights are the seeds of new learning. New learning is required to deal with complexity. And complexity is what we've got. If we don't stop, we don't have a chance.

We fool ourselves into thinking we can outrun the unknowns. We can't.

We trick ourselves into thinking that our speed of completion is our greatest value. It's not.

We mistakenly equate activity with productivity, thinking our checklist is a path to purpose. It isn't.

In a world of "go" it's those who "stop" who will notice what's needed for the way forward. At the dawn of the age of meaning, the new currency is learning. Invest wisely.

And don't forget to breathe.

Author's note: In an embarrassing coincidence, I realize that I wrote this post exactly one year before getting lost in the woods on Whidbey Island. As author Anne Lamott once wrote, "The road to enlightenment is long, bring snacks and magazines."

THE SPACE BETWEEN

{November 27, 2013}

We are always leaving behind and we are always moving towards. We are always losing and always gaining.

Between grief and thankfulness there is a space. That space is today.

Yesterday we buried my mother-in-law, committing to the earth a woman who is remembered for her sparkle and her sass, her practical goodness and her deep love of family. My wife, with the strength and composure that are her signature gifts, represented the family with a eulogy that reminded us that her mom's death was no tragedy, coming as it did after a long struggle with Alzheimer's.

Our grief is as much for Marion's death as it is for the years we lost to a disease so merciless in its thievery of the simple joys of recognition, remembrance and connection.

Tomorrow we will share in a Thanksgiving feast, the preparations for which are already underway. We will celebrate our family, near and far. We will celebrate our opportunities and our relationships. We will be mindful of how much – and it is so, so much – we have and, perhaps in that recognition make a new resolution to share it more generously than we have before.

And what about this space between? What about today?

Between the depths of our grief and the height of our thankfulness we live another day, both replete and unremarkable. Like every day, it contains all of it. Whether we choose to see or acknowledge it, it is with us, the losses we mourn, the gifts we celebrate. All are contained in this single day.

We are always leaving behind and we are always moving towards. We are always losing and always gaining.

This space between? This is now.

And it holds everything.

GROWN UP

{February 12, 2014}

What they don't understand about birthdays and what they
never tell you is that when you're eleven, you're also ten,
and nine, and eight, and seven, and six, and five, and four,
and three, and two, and one. And when you wake up on your
eleventh birthday you expect to feel eleven, but you don't. You
open your eyes and everything's just like yesterday, only it's
today. And you don't feel eleven at all. You feel like you're still
ten. And you are—underneath the year that makes you eleven.

– Sandra Cisneros

I felt like a grown up last week. I had a new experience – hosting a
leadership conference – and it went well. It made me feel the accumulated
confidence of my experience. It helped me to recognize my capability and
to be gratified by the opportunity to express it in a useful way; in a way that
helped others gain more from the conference than they might otherwise
have done.

In that moment of feeling "grown up" – like how Doug Silsbee so
artfully uses the metaphor of a dragon tail as a "felt sense of fundamental sufficiency" – I recognized how often it is that I don't feel that way.
I recognized how often it is that younger versions of me – the uncertain
23-year-old, the confused 10-year-old, the insecure 35-year-old, the play-
fully confident 16-year-old, the naively curious 5-year-old – emerge and
express themselves. And why shouldn't they? I've been all of those ages
much longer than I've been 43. Those patterns, expressions, beliefs and
behaviors are well practiced and well worn. They just aren't definitive. As
the next layer forms the previous one is flattened out, diminished by the
weight of what's next.

I'd like to feel "grown up" more often but I have no desire to forget the best parts of being 23, 35, 16 and 5. I want to hold onto the value of uncertainty, embrace the questions of confusion, wrestle with the insecurity of new experience, relish in the playfulness of confident presence and learn with the naive fervor of an innocent child.

The story is still being written, as long as it is. I bring all of it with me.

INEVITABLE

{March 25, 2014}

John Cage said that fear in life is the fear of change. If I may add to that: nothing can avoid changing. It's the only thing you can count on. Because life doesn't have any other possibility, everyone can be measured by his adaptability to change.

– Robert Rauschenberg

I recently asked a group of adults, to support them in gaining clarity about the kind of leader they wanted to be, how they would like to be remembered. It didn't go over well. It seems that our common mortality is not a great conversation starter.

Leaders who are well equipped for change operate with the confidence and clarity that comes from having perspective. That perspective, put simply, is this: Everything changes. Everything ends.

We are creatures of the natural world – all the electronic trappings and conveniences aside – organic beings with an opportunity to distinguish ourselves unlike any other organic beings with which we share our tiny planet. But, we are organic just the same and, as such, destined to complete the cycle of life. For those of us lucky enough to live in circumstances that allow us to do so – with enough clean water, food, energy, services, employment – the only question we have to face is how we want it to go. We don't even have to face that question, of course. Many, many people choose not to: blessed with circumstances and opportunities that millions of others don't have, they are ambivalent about their own existence and just bob along through life moving toward the inevitability of its end. But, since this is a blog for leaders, influencers and agents of change, I choose not to get lost down the rabbit hole of that particular tragedy.

As I get ready to complete my 44th year a couple of weeks from now, I recognize with some ambitious calculation that I am at the halfway point of my life. Since the "average" American male can expect to live to age 77, it is generous for me to consider myself at the midpoint. Just for fun – and because I'm in no hurry – I'm considering this optimistically and giving myself credit for a healthy lifestyle and good longevity in the gene pool, at least on my mom's side. If I am fortunate enough to avoid a fatal disease or a tragic accident, maybe, just maybe, I can make it to age 88; another 44 years of quality life.

Here's what I believe will sustain me in LIVING the next 44 years well AND in full awareness of the 100% certainty of my life coming to an end. Maybe it will work for you, too:

1. My vocation: I'm doing the work I am supposed to do and from here on out I will creatively explore the limits of my potential in living into that work as fully as I can.

2. The sustaining power of family, friendship and community matters more to me now than ever before. I am learning at a foundational level, despite my well-worn tendency to "go it alone," that there are many, many people who support, embrace and encourage my journey. I am both indebted to their generosity and committed to reciprocating as best I can.

3. Clear values and purpose: There is nothing that has impacted the trajectory of my life more positively than getting clear about what I stand for, getting clear about the purposeful intention of my life and then experiencing the daily challenge of living into it and up to it. It is both humbling and invigorating and I am grateful for those who helped me figure it out.

Yes, everything changes and everything ends. Between now and then is all the time we need.

WONDER

{April 8, 2014}

Men go abroad to wonder at the heights of mountains, at the huge waves of the sea, at the long courses of the rivers, at the vast compass of the ocean, at the circular motions of the stars, and they pass by themselves without wondering.

– Saint Augustine

Any distraction from ourselves will do, it seems. Anything that allows us to justify an external rather than an internal focus. Of course the "heights of mountains" and the "huge waves of the sea" are more compelling, we tell ourselves, unwilling as we so often are to recognize the mountains and waves within us, peaking and forming in support of the infrastructure that is our life. Our whole life.

That life is lived both on the mountaintops and in the valleys; both on the crests of the waves and in the hollow spaces between them. I don't need to tell you that, of course. You know too well what it feels like to experience those darker, flatter, hollowed-out feelings. As do I.

I am simply reminding myself to live more fully into both the light and the shadow of my existence. To develop an even greater curiosity about what is going on inside as I feel myself engaging with the world; high and low, good and bad, mountain top and valley floor.

When we choose to be cartographers of our inner landscape we develop the capacity to navigate our experience with the confidence of awareness; with the thoughtfulness of a seasoned traveler.

Coming alive to ourselves we might just spark a sense of wonder that says, "Look at all that I am!"

IF YOU CHOOSE TO LIVE AN UNEXAMINED LIFE PLEASE INFLICT IT ON SOMEBODY ELSE.

—Parker Palmer

REFLECTIVE

{April 24, 2014}

The theme this month at my daughter's school is "Reflective." They are teaching the children to value and practice the discipline of looking within.

They are planting seeds now that have the potential, with thoughtful cultivation, to bloom into a lifelong commitment to build personal capacity through self-knowledge. The implications are massive.

Our organizations today teem with leaders who do not possess the ability or the inclination to look within. They have either never been introduced to reflective practices or, if they have, they have decided that they are too soft and immeasurable for the "real world." In my opinion, this is defensive reasoning to protect themselves from what they might experience in a real encounter with the person who exists under their carefully managed facade. Because they haven't dug out any interior space, they lack the capacity to deal with complexity, change and the general messiness of the human and organizational experience. As a result, when their bucket gets full, the parts they can't effectively "hold" slosh out onto everyone around them, resulting in anger, contempt, distraction, disruption and the feeding of fear.

Parker Palmer has said, riffing on Socrates, "if you choose to live an unexamined life please inflict it on somebody else."

It may be that the greatest gift we can give our children is the gift of a reflective discipline. This is, I believe, the only hope for the future of our organizations, places that hold the promise of providing us with the opportunity to fulfill the meaning and purpose of our lives. To give this gift, however, requires that we start with ourselves.

There's still plenty of daylight. Why not grab a shovel and get to work?

DOWN TO THE STUDS

{June 10, 2014}

What's more disruptive over time is not the confrontation required to bring about meaningful change but the damage caused by pretending you don't need to.

Sometimes in life you recognize that what you're experiencing – the change you're being called to make, the recognition that this is no longer how you want to be – won't be handled by another paint job, a new appliance or a different wallpaper.

Sometimes you realize that you've got to take it all the way down to the studs and start again.

And you don't want to. Because it's messier, no doubt about it. You might find mold. Or water damage. Or termites. And when you find it, you'll have to deal with it. And that means more disruption, more time and more expense.

What's more disruptive over time is not the confrontation required to bring about meaningful change but the damage caused by pretending you don't need to.

You can tinker all you like. Sooner or later it just won't be enough.

HIS COURAGEOUS
LOOK WITHIN MADE
THE DIFFERENCE
BETWEEN A LIFE
PLAGUED BY
DOUBT AND ONE
EMBOLDENED BY
AWARENESS.

A MODEL MANAGER

{August 25, 2014}

Joe Torre was inducted into the Major League Baseball Hall of Fame earlier this summer and just this weekend his number six was retired by the New York Yankees. He is, by any definition, one of the great baseball men of the last century. By my estimation, he's just one of the great men. Period.

I have never been nor will I likely ever be a Yankees fan. But I respect greatness and I respect the leadership that leads to greatness. Joe Torre is a tremendous model of the truism that you must first lead yourself before you can effectively lead others. It is no coincidence that his moment of revelation in 1995, a moment in which he courageously opened himself to the pain of insight that leads to understanding, marked the beginning of a shift in his leadership impact.

In a New York Times piece by Tyler Kepner, Torre candidly discussed his realization that there was an incredibly important, deeply hurtful source of self-doubt that had prevented him from believing in himself the way so many others did. Growing up in an abusive household, he felt responsible, as kids so often do, for the pain of something over which he had no control.

"So I started talking about it, which people don't do, even to this day. Once I realized I wasn't born with these feelings of being inferior, which is the way I categorized them, I was excited. Because now I found out that, 'O.K., I'm normal like everybody else.' I just had something that — and not that I'm blaming my father — but at least I knew that this was created as I was a kid growing up. So it was a freedom to talk about it because I could just say, 'Hey, yeah, this went on in my life.'"

Torre added later:

> "*I had friends growing up who had no clue what was going on in my house. And I didn't want to share it. I was embarrassed by it, and I thought I caused it because there was a lot of whispering in my house. So finding out all these things weren't true, it was sort of like you wanted to shout it from the rooftops.*"

His willingness to finally look into this darkest corner opened up the freedom to discover a new, more accurate version of himself, one that matched the person so many others easily saw.

In addition to winning four World Series with the Yankees, Torre's legacy will be defined by his leadership off the field. His foundation, Safe at Home, provides safe rooms for children impacted by violence in the home. Fifty thousand children have benefited from the program so far.

Mr. Kepner's piece concluded this way:

> *The calming presence in the corner of the dugout, the master clubhouse communicator, the charming public figure, all of those roles were hard earned for Torre. The steward of baseball's last true dynasty has a permanent place in Yankees lore and a deeper, more important legacy than he ever could have imagined in 1995.*

Joe Torre met the possibility of his future once he made peace with the truth of his past. His courageous look within made the difference between a life plagued by doubt and one emboldened by awareness. We desperately need his example.

And we desperately need many more just like him. Will you be among them?

HERE

{October 17, 2014}

Traveler, there is no path.
The path is made by walking.

– Antonio Machado

I came across a mushroom growing out of the moss, which had grown into the space between the boards of an everyday picnic bench. It was very, very small. Later that evening it rained for a long time.

The next day I went back to the bench to check on the mushroom. It was gone.

I wish I saw the moss between the cracks as the solid ground on which I long to stand.

I wish I could say that "this" is enough: that I will start from right here; that I do not see the bench and that I do not see the ground, that I do not see the rain clouds forming or feel the unsteady vibrations of weathered wood coming undone.

What if I could only see the green, velvety wellspring of possibility holding up my own smallness, feeding it and urging it to grow, grow, grow?

The rain is coming. Always.

There was a small mushroom on a picnic bench, growing out of the moss in the space between the wood.

THE BIGGEST
LEADERSHIP MISTAKE
IS GETTING IN THE
WAY OF WHAT IS
ALREADY THERE.

DON'T MOTIVATE ME, PLEASE

{December 14, 2014}

People are internally motivated. The good work of leadership is to tap into that motivation and accelerate, support, deepen and encourage it. I think the biggest leadership mistake is getting in the way of what is already there. It is the hubris of thinking that I either have to supply motivation or that my version of it is superior to what someone brings with them. This is classically paternalistic. "That's nice," says the well-intentioned leader, "but here's how it should be."

So many employees buy into this paternalism because they love the protection it affords. They are making a painful trade-off by accepting someone else's version of how they should feel, think and believe and only because one rung on the pay scale separates them. At best, this substitution of perspective is an ill-fitting replacement, and at worst, it's deeply corrosive.

The courageous leadership move is toward a partnership that is about maximizing what the individual has to offer; what you saw in them in the first place that made you want to hire them.

Leaders control, in my opinion, because the chaos of the individual is just too overwhelming. That is to say, most leaders don't seem to have the capacity to treat each individual employee as a naturally, uniquely motivated person and figure out how to make the most of what they have to offer. That capacity doesn't exist because the leader hasn't looked within long enough or purposefully enough to discover their own motivation.

Ultimately, they just end up repeating the pattern of their experience because they haven't learned to value and express their personal, internal perspective. Instead, the leader lumps everyone together, expecting them to be "just like me" and thinking that somehow this is going to lead to innovation and value creation.

How can it possibly?

Start within. The courageous step is the one back to yourself.

THE DOOR OF INTEGRITY

{December 30, 2014}

The more coherent one becomes within oneself as a creature, the more one fully enters into the communion of all creatures.

– Wendell Berry

The sign above my daughter's classroom door reads as follows:

THE DOOR OF INTEGRITY:

I am responsible for everything
I think, say, do and feel.

This is Viktor Frankl's challenge to us when he writes, "Between stimulus and response there is a space. In that space is our power to choose our response. In our response lies our growth and our freedom."

And, I would add, in our response lies our integrity, the evidence of our more or less cohesive self.

How incredible that we get to choose! We, alone among creatures, have the opportunity to reflect on our impulses and find even more effective ways to interact with the world. Wendell Berry reminds us that this effort is never for its own sake but that the deepening of personal understanding is at once the strengthening of connection with everyone and everything around us.

Yes, we get to choose and it is even more extraordinary when we – when I – actually do.

May the happiness, the prosperity, the failure and the learning you experience in the coming year be marked by your deepest possible experience of integrity. However difficult it may be to swallow in the moment, may the aftertaste of personal responsibility be a savory accompaniment to the freedom you will have so rightly earned.

The best thing about the "Door of Integrity" is that we can all squeeze through.

Let's meet on the other side.

THE WELL

{February 12, 2015}

The purpose of the inward journey is to ready ourselves for the outward expression of our very best selves.

Reach way over, toes keeping contact with earth, hips balanced on the rough edge, arm stretching down to break the surface of the water. Dip your cup and taste your presence.

This is your well, the internal spring of all that you are and all that you have to offer a waiting world.

Don't drink from other wells, mistaking them for your own. Drink from your well, the one that is hardest to reach, the bottom of which is furthest from your hand. Reach down through the darkness to find a quenching you can find nowhere else.

You will love what you taste with a sadness for having not tasted it long or often enough.

Drink it in. Supply yourself for what you must give away.

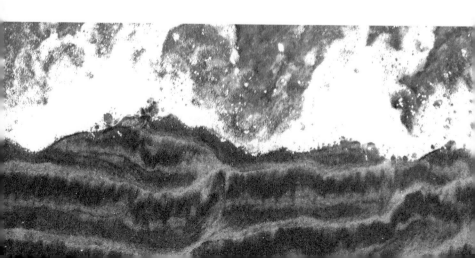

SAND AND WATER

{March 17, 2015}

There is a reliable constancy of change. Our opportunity is
to stay open and aware of how we influence it and how it
influences us.

You are both sand and water.

You are forming and being formed, the ultimate collaboration.

When you accept the continuous reality of your deeply potent change-
ability, you create space for beauty you couldn't otherwise imagine. Your
agency intact, you invite the possibility that comes with each new wave.

There is design in the chaos, intricate and purposeful. Each new surge
offers its contribution to the work in progress that you are. You will grow
weary of their insistence; how could you not? And the waves will keep
coming, persistently offering an invitation to a "more" that frightens with
its sincerity.

The water is never just washing over. It is always forming something new.

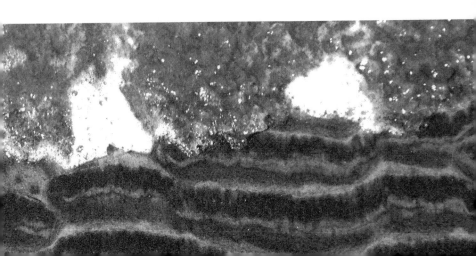

Q: HOW DO YOU
KNOW YOU'RE ON
THE RIGHT PATH?

A: IT'S THE HARD ONE

Q & A

{March 20, 2015}

Q: How did you end up here?
A: I chose to come.

Q: How did you decide?
A: It made the most sense to me at the time. It appealed to my values and my strengths. It held the possibility of both creative and financial reward.

Q: Did you have any doubts?
A: Of course. Certainty is overrated. It's an immature reaction to the fear of the unknown.

Q: What would you tell someone in a similar position?
A: To get clear on who they are before getting clear on what they want. And to trust themselves, above all.

Q: Do you have any regrets?
A: Yes. I regret that I didn't act sooner. I regret that I avoided my heart's desire out of fear of failure, perfectionism, feeling out of control. And, I am here now.

Q: How did you overcome those things?
A: I didn't. I minimized them so they don't take up as much space. They will always be there.

Q: What frightens you?
A: My narcissism. It seduces me into thinking that I deserve things that actually require hard work.

Q: What do you pine for?

A: First, to feel profound satisfaction for all that I have. Second, for the courage to keep moving towards an even greater contribution.

Q: How do you know you're on the right path?

A: It's the hard one.

Q: That doesn't sound very fun.

A: I know. And there's not a day on the right path that isn't full of joyful possibility. It's an extraordinary paradox.

Q: I get a feeling of isolation or deep independence in talking with you.

A: You feel that accurately. I have always struggled to "use" others well. It comes from a feeling of having something to prove, I think. Rationally, I understand the power and importance of relationship but emotionally I allow myself to separate, thinking I've got to go it alone. It's a sharp edge for me.

Q: How are you working on it, if you don't mind my asking?

A: I don't mind. I remind myself to be focused and present with the person in front of me right now and to trust the reciprocal nature of relationship. That means starting close in, right at home, with my wife and my children.

Q: What's next for you?

A: To keep moving forward. Everything is a choice. I will keep making the best ones I can.

HOLDING

{March 25, 2015}

We are not intended to overcome our resistance to change. We are intended to stay in conversation with it. That conversation is the source of our greatest possibility.

I walked outside after our last rainfall. I think I was going to check for the mail. I found this.

More and more I find myself attracted to the fragile and the tenuous. I am drawn to what will not last; the temporary, the changing, the transitory.

I am the drop of water, sliding off with the next breeze, evaporating into the warming air. I am a small child longing to become. I am a contribution hoping to be made.

Some days I want to stay on the leaf, holding out hope that it will remain just like this for just a little longer. Some days I am ready to get soaked in, nourishment for something greater.

Being held is best appreciated in the letting go.

...YOUR LEADERSHIP
EFFECTIVENESS IS
DETERMINED BY HOW
WELL YOU KNOW
YOURSELF AND BY
HOW EFFECTIVELY
YOU APPLY THAT
KNOWLEDGE WITH
AND FOR THOSE
YOU LEAD.

WHO YOU ARE

{April 13, 2015}

"Who you are" is not necessarily a question to be answered nor is it a problem to be solved. Rather it is an incremental, sometimes dramatic understanding to live into, deepen and shape as life progresses. One way to think about it that has been particularly useful to me is to consider my common or default response to other people when I am under stress. More and more, psychologist Karen Horney's work has been essential to this awareness, opening up a channel through which to better understand my reactions that then gives me the opportunity to make different choices.

If you lead other people, I believe you must do this work. Use the language below to get started and then go validate your impressions by gathering feedback from those you lead. If that's too big a stretch right now, start smaller with those who know you best and from whom you are willing and able to hear the truth. It is a simple and powerful equation: your leadership effectiveness is determined by how well you know yourself and by how effectively you apply that knowledge with and for those you lead.

Under stress, do you:

Move away from people? Do you disappear, choosing to go it alone and handle things your own way because of your need to get it just right? Do you steer away from chaos or complexity because the lack of control you feel is overwhelming and disarming?

This is the leader who shuts the door, relying only on herself to find the "perfect" solution to the problem.

Move toward people? Do you become compliant, seeking the approval of others as a way to avoid confrontation? Do you fit in and follow expecting others to solve the problems you face?

This is the leader who asks everyone for ideas, especially his boss, in his desperation to disperse ownership of the problem.

Move against people? Do you exert control and power, using others to get what you want with little regard for their needs? Do you go after achievement at all costs and expect recognition for your efforts?

This is the leader who leaps into action, controlling people like chess pieces in a game of "win or lose."

All leaders, all people, have a default position under the pressure of anxiety and stress. When you find yours, you begin to break free from the rigidity of an old pattern. You start to develop the fluidity of choice necessary to be the leader your team needs you to be.

LEARNING AT THE SPEED OF CHANGE

{April 16, 2015}

If the journey is toward a richer inner life...we're best served by establishing our own speed limit.

I drove over 300 miles yesterday, up to Los Angeles in the morning to meet one client and back to San Diego in the afternoon to meet another. It's not a schedule I'd like to make a habit of, but time on the road has its advantages. Phone calls and podcasts are welcome companions. This morning in the quiet stillness of a more typical day it's remarkable to me that I could have so easily covered that much distance just a day ago.

In the pre-railroad 1800s, intrepid families heading west covered 10-20 miles a day in horse-drawn wagons. You can walk faster than that! It must have been exhilarating, even at such a modest pace, to be headed into the unknown, but they weren't exactly racing there.

And perhaps that's worth thinking about.

At 15 miles per hour, the early settlers probably noticed an awful lot of detail about their surroundings as they plodded along. In the slow rhythm of their progress, they had plenty of time to consider both the possibilities and pitfalls of their endeavor. At 75 miles per hour, I noticed many other cars, the freeway, the Pacific Ocean, Orange County, Los Angeles County and the Hollywood sign. I saw my alma mater on the hill and noticed a plane taking off from LAX. I took in a macro perspective while the incalculable details of everyday life were lost on me.

If the journey is toward a richer inner life, a more astute personal awareness, we're best served by establishing our own speed limit. Am I advocating that we slow down, cover less ground and take more in? I suppose so, yes. And not just because that's a healthy and necessary antidote to the seduction of an otherwise punishing pace. My notion is that the internal journey – the frontier conversation with ourselves – is not very inviting, nor is it really even possible at more than a wagon's pace. The idea of racing towards deeper understanding implies that we would only see the landmarks, the obvious and impossible-to-miss truths about who we are. While they are important, they only represent the beginning of the conversation, a natural place to start. I saw the Hollywood sign but I don't know anything more about Hollywood.

Your local flavor, the parts of you that need to be seen if they are to be understood, requires a different pace, one that is in service of a deeper kind of knowing.

DEVELOPING YOUR VOICE OF UNDERSTANDING

A well-developed Voice of Understanding is one that can articulate a clear narrative or storyline about the self. These are the areas I have explored to piece together that narrative into something I can work with more concretely. When it became clear that my impact would be proportionate to my understanding, I needed answers and explanations that took me further. I found them, in part, through an exploration of these elements:

- CORE VALUES: What you believe in. How you decide to spend your time and money.

- STRENGTHS: How you excel. What others have learned to count on in you.

- PURPOSE: What you are here to do.

- ASPIRATIONS: Your specific personal and professional goals.

- PREFERENCES: How you show up in the world when you are operating from your true or core self.

- WEAKNESSES: How you typically get yourself into trouble.

- EDUCATION: What you know and how you came to know it.

- WORK EXPERIENCE: Lessons learned by earning a living.

– SIGNIFICANT LIFE EVENTS: What you've done and what has happened to you that paved the way from there to here.

– FAMILY INFLUENCE: The impact of your family of origin, the role you played and the events that took place there.

Some of these things – values, strengths and preferences – can be discovered through any number of tools and assessments, many of which are free and can be found online. I would call that "level one" of your exploration. It is essential but not sufficient.

"Level two" requires deeper study. It's a process not just of identification but also of interpretation. As you start to dig into your life events and family relationships, it is extremely helpful, and oftentimes necessary, to have the support of an experienced and trusted advisor. This could be an excellent mentor, a professional coach, or a licensed therapist. There is no "right" way to go about this kind of deeper learning. There is, I think, a quality of commitment required that is about seeking and discovering an accurate version of your story so that it becomes usable to you in a new way. In the spirit of the voices of connection and exploration still to come, that commitment requires a willingness to move towards the edge and a position of openness to the support of those who can help you do so safely and productively.

PART II

THE VOICE OF CONNECTION

YOUR GREAT MISTAKE IS TO ACT THE DRAMA AS IF YOU WERE ALONE.

- David Whyte

INTRODUCTION

One summer, not long ago, I took my daughters fishing for the first time. It was early June as we stood on the shore of a picturesque mountain lake. After furnishing our simple rods and reels with sinkers, bobbers, hooks and bait, I handed one to each of the girls and encouraged them to be patient. Within five minutes, each had hooked and landed a fish. Instant gratification. Smiles (and disbelief) all around.

One girl, beaming with pride, inspected every inch of her fish. The other squirmed away from the scene more than happy to have me take care of the dirty work. In the jubilation of our sudden success and in the many retellings that would follow, I would have benefited from George Bernard Shaw's admonition that "Success covers a multitude of blunders." It was another year before I would fully understand what he meant.

The following summer in late July we returned to the same spot. I assembled our gear just as before and again handed each girl a fully outfitted fishing pole. We were more than ready for the same result. Those lines went in the water with some very high expectations along for the ride.

This time, not so fast.

I remember thinking that it was some kind of cosmic payback, our quick and easy success the year before meaning we would be tested this time around. Not to worry, I assured them: our moment would come. This was a learning opportunity, a chance to practice patience. It was a much more realistic introduction to the world of fishing.

Sitting near us along the lake's edge were two women, a mother and daughter who were having a great time doing something that, each time it happened, never failed to get our attention. They were catching fish. These two were more than a little rough around the edges, noticeable from both their appearance and their conversation. What stood out about them was the way they wore their fishing licenses in plastic cases attached to lanyards around their necks. The only other place I had seen this was at Disneyland where the most fanatical park-goers wear their annual passes in just the same way and adorn them with all kinds of pins and buttons. It speaks of a certain kind of commitment, a statement of a more intimate awareness than that of the casual visitor.

It must have been tough for them to endure our futility. After about an hour, one of the women nudged her Powerbait container towards me and said "They're likin' the green today."

"Oh, thank you," I said, immediately recognizing in her generosity my resistance to the offer. I reluctantly tried it out with no success. In the meantime, they kept on catching fish.

A few minutes later I noticed a man to our left pack up his gear and begin what I thought was the walk to his car. Instead, he headed directly for us. Here was help again, I assumed correctly, and here was my resistance rushing in before he had said a word.

"Hello," I offered as he made his way closer.

"Hi," he said. And then, matter of factly, "I sure would like to see your kids catch some fish."

"You and me both," I blurted right back.

"Do you mind if I take a look at your set-up?" he continued.

"Sure," I replied and then I stammered out the disbelief and frustration I had been feeling all afternoon. "I just don't understand it! When we here last summer we just dropped the lines in the water and caught some fish!"

"When were you here?" he asked. The question drew a blank stare. Its relevance was beyond me.

"It was early June," I finally said.

"Well, it's late July now," came his response, confident that he had settled the matter.

Unable to mask my ignorance I said, "So?"

"The water is warmer now."

At this point, I wanted to scream, "Please just tell me what the hell is going on!" but I just said, "And?"

"Trout are cold-water fish. When the water warms up during the summer, they go where the cold water is, to the bottom of the lake. You have a bobber on your line that is keeping your hook near the surface. That makes sense in early June but not in late July."

All at once I noticed that not one other person fishing that lake had a bobber on their line. I couldn't see it before. I had no vision for it.

He continued, "If you don't mind, I'll reset your lines with some heavier weights and some smaller hooks. Your bait is fine, you just need to put it where the fish are."

A complete stranger took the time to educate and equip us, using his own supplies, to do what we had come there to do. Over the next hour or so we practiced casting our lines into deeper water, and the effort paid off. We caught five rainbow and brown trout that afternoon.

I felt the oddest combination of shame and gratitude, disappointment and achievement. We had gotten what we came for but at the steep price of my realization that I was the reason it had taken us so long to do so. I was a prisoner of my experience, and I didn't know it, could not see it and was, sadly, unable and unwilling to try.

For an hour and a half, we sat next to not one, but two expert fishermen and all I could do was grudgingly accept their offer of bait. I knew those lanyards – along with all of those caught fish – meant local knowledge and experience but I couldn't even muster a simple request for help. My prejudice and my stubbornness got in the way. That is a tough combination, especially for someone who desperately needs to learn something new! They were different. Rough around the edges, remember? I let that blind me to their obvious expertise.

Not until someone offered me clear and direct feedback did the bubble of my conceit finally break. That bubble held the disbelief that my approach was not working. That bubble held my certainty that based on one previous successful experience I knew enough to do it again. That bubble held my commitment to the past and none of my attention to the present. Seduced by a single version of success, I easily disallowed the possibility that another solution – another person's experience – might not just be viable, but necessary.

To my untrained eye, the lake was exactly the same place one year later. Since the biggest change was an invisible one, a greater demand was placed on a new way of seeing. My biggest opportunity on that second day at the lake was to connect with those who could teach me, to hold a beginner's mindset and to say "yes" to all I still needed to learn.

More Human than Otherwise

There is help everywhere. And not just help, but brilliance. Our job as leaders is to see it and engage it, but so often our egos get in the way. We have to be right, to be in control, to prove that we know what to do and how to do it. After all, isn't that why we got the job? Through our relentless need for independent achievement, we are often more willing to exhaust ourselves than to connect with others and allow them to help us.

We all want and need meaningful connection. Even though there are plenty of days we would like to try, we know we can't go it alone. It's just that connection can be messy: it creates feelings of vulnerability and sometimes doesn't work out the way we'd like it to. And it is precisely that messiness that we need to wade into if we are going to find the common ground – the shared experience – that makes meaningful relationship the foundation of so much extraordinary achievement.

Everyone has a compelling story, a stormy past, a crazy family, a travel nightmare, a heroic moment, a childlike fascination, core strengths they want to use and values they want to live out. Any other human being willing enough to inquire about these things in a thoughtful way can become a catalyst for their expression. By doing so, we forge connections that lead to intimacy and trust.

When someone offers a sincere invitation to know us and to be known, something changes in the quality of our interaction. We are no longer co-workers transacting another in an endless line of tasks or agreements but partners committed to one another's success. This is where the more territorial strategic mind yields some ground to the open heart. It is the meeting place for both the logical demands of efficiency and the beautifully illogical demands of just being a human in a confusing world.

The Voice of Connection calls us to risk ourselves in the endeavor of human relationship. It harkens us to a belief that our leadership "power" comes less from positional authority and more from human similarity. The more we share what is unfinished about ourselves – what we're learning, how we struggle, what we aspire to – the more we normalize for others the unfinished parts of themselves. After all, the ultimate power of connection is that many "unfinished" people can come together and complement one another in service of accomplishing great things. How else does it happen?

When we embrace the truth that we are all "more human than otherwise" (Sullivan, 1968), we gain both the humility and the confidence to share the best of ourselves and gain access to the best parts of others. We are privileged to experience those human qualities that are most worthy of protection: creative spirit, innocence, curiosity and reservoirs of energy and commitment that bring engagement to new heights. These so often remain hidden because they are too important to share with anyone who is not worthy of them. I've heard it said that the worst thing you can say to someone who is nervous about speaking in public is to "just be yourself." It goes to our greatest fear that the more of our true selves we reveal, the more we risk the best of us being rejected. If that should happen, what then?

I struggled with this for years and years, putting on an air of sufficiency, standing out as much as possible, as boldly as possible, to distract from the possibility of being truly known. To know me would have been to see an insecure, perfectionistic person unwilling to connect because of the real danger of failing by comparison. My experience of relationship became polarized. In many cases, I kept my distance, hungry for the reciprocity of authentic connection but afraid of the cost. At other times, I would smother the person I cared about to make sure they wouldn't discard me, which of course, left them no choice but to do just that. In all of this either/or, I missed out on the best part of relationships for fear of experiencing the worst. You'll see this struggle reflected in the selections that follow, my progressions and regressions in the nonlinear reality of human relationships.

I am still learning about connection and my consolation in doing so is to remember that, yes, we are all more human than otherwise. It is the only starting point we need to activate the *Voice of Connection.*

WHAT I'M REALLY WONDERING IS IF I CAN BE THE LEADER THAT I NEED TO BE TO KEEP THINGS GOING STRONG...

HOW MUCH CREAM CHEESE?

{August 31, 2009}

...Rationally, I believe so. Emotionally? Well, that's probably why I start to hold on just a little too tightly.

For a long time now I've been espousing the importance of personal disclosure and vulnerability as key leadership traits. I've thought, talked and written at length about the importance of showing up more "fully human" because that's the kind of person people want to follow. Recently, I had the chance to experience firsthand just how much this matters and it how it can ground us in our relationships in ways otherwise not attainable.

A year, maybe a year-and-a-half ago, I shared with some colleagues a story that perfectly describes my style under stress. When I feel out of control, uncertain, or unstable, my tendency is to over-control. As you'll see, I'm not just talking about micromanaging, but about getting intense about stuff, really small stuff, that just doesn't merit that kind of energy or attention. I've been doing this for a VERY long time and, thankfully, in the last few years I've started to notice the behavior and, as I hope those close to me will attest, started to change it.

A few years back on a Saturday morning my wife and I took the kids to a bagel shop for breakfast. My son, probably six or seven at the time, had smeared so much cream cheese on his bagel that there was no longer any bagel. It was piled high! Control freak and hyper-intense parent that I was, I promptly grabbed the bagel from him and began to deconstruct it. I quickly removed the most offensive glob and then I proceeded to take one of those plastic serrated knives and scrape it clean. The only thing left on this bagel was the tracks of the knife through what may or may not have been a pile of cream cheese.

The look my wife gave me was of utter disbelief. After a painful silence, we just started laughing. What I had done was just so bad, so clearly over-the-top, that all you could do was laugh about it. I don't know what was going on with me then, why exactly I needed to exert so much control over bagel-to-cream cheese ratios. Most likely, I was still in the early stages of learning how to see myself honestly and feeling the need to control the mess that that kind of examination creates.

I told this story to a group of colleagues about 18 months ago as a way to describe my ongoing challenge with control needs. Just last week, one of these colleagues came to my office and expressed concern about how I was approaching an issue in our group. It was clear that she was feeling the weight of my control and, to illustrate her point, she somewhat tentatively reminded me of the bagel story. It was a beautiful moment. Her recollection of the anecdote was perfectly timed to coincide with what's true for me right now.

As I've written about recently, I'm in the middle of a big transition right now. My boss left our organization, his replacement is in place and I'm trying to find my way through the sometimes muddy and unsettled waters that go with such change. Is it any wonder that I would respond by holding on a little too tightly, exerting just a little too much control? If I had never shared the bagel story, my colleague could never have helped me gain the perspective I needed to move through this change more effectively. She brought back to me the thing I had given her, returning it to me so I could look at it with fresh eyes and new learning. What a gift!

The truth is, there's a lot at stake right now. Lots of opportunity for me to ensure that, in the absence of an influential leader, our work continues to grow and thrive. What I'm really wondering is if I can be the leader that I need to be to keep things going strong. Rationally, I believe so. Emotionally? Well, that's probably why I start to hold on just a little too tightly.

Frankly, I think it's a good time to hold on a little tighter, to make sure what we've got going here isn't all cream cheese and no bagel. The good news is, as I have been so freshly reminded, that I'm better equipped to notice my tendency to reach for the plastic knife.

TEAM SPIRIT

{August 31, 2009}

When you ask people...what it is like being part of a great team, what is most striking is the meaningfulness of the experience, people talk about being part of something larger than themselves, of being connected, of being generative. It becomes quite clear that, for many, their experiences as part of truly great teams stand out as singular periods of life lived to the fullest. Some spend the rest of their lives looking for ways to recapture that spirit.

– Peter Senge

When I was in college I had the single greatest team experience of my life. I was a member of the men's chorus at Loyola Marymount University under the demanding and deeply meaningful direction of Paul Salamunovich, truly a master of choral conducting. Coming out of high school I was the embodiment of the "big fish" who had been swimming around in the small pond of choral music and theater. I had a lot of natural musicality, but I wasn't much of a "technical" musician and my audition to join the choral program at LMU was an abrupt and unsettling reality check. I recall Mr. Salamunovich at one point saying to me: "You do know it's important to actually do the exercises I am asking you to do, right?" This was a much bigger ocean than I realized.

Once I got my sea legs, I knew I had become a part of something truly special. Rehearsals were intense and fun, the music was challenging and gorgeous, and the camaraderie was the best type of "male bonding." We were silly and juvenile until the downbeat came and then it was the best of musical professionalism and integrity. The most memorable part was how I learned to be a part of a group within a group and to own the results of my work, both good and bad. As you likely know, a choral group is typically made up of at least four sections, with each section responsible for learning its part and then integrating that part into the whole. This demands study and practice and then a ton of listening to truly get it right. Done well, and all four of those parts (sometimes six and even eight) sound like they are coming from one voice. When that is achieved it can be a moving experience for the listener. I know it's a transcendent experience for the singers. And, we got there many, many times in the three years I was privileged to be a part of this group.

In the years following college, because my membership on this incredible team had been so singular, it was years before I even considered joining another group. When I did, I was mostly dissatisfied with the experience because it didn't and couldn't measure up. This was troubling for me because of how much I love to sing. My standards and expectations had risen so high that I frequently felt like I was settling for "second best."

Is it worth it to have a peak experience even if might spoil you for future endeavors? I think it is. It bestows an embodied awareness of possibility that can be translated, if not with the same results, to new scenarios in which people are committed to creating something meaningful. After all, those peak experiences are as much about the connecting and the striving together – let's call that the process – as they are about the outcomes. To further the point, I don't remember anything about our audiences through the years but I remember the names and faces of scores of my peers, the tour experiences and home stays we shared, the goofy pranks on long bus rides and all of the in-between "stuff" that made it such a rich experience.

Most of all, I remember rehearsals in the choir room and the peak experiences that we shared together – no audience in sight – week after week as we strived, groaned, laughed and created together. One of my roommates used to come and listen to our rehearsals. He was a smart guy. It's where we did some of our very best work.

Today, I'm less concerned with finding "ways to recapture that spirit" as Senge describes it above and far more interested in testing my own willingness to show up in a spirit of possibility to all endeavors in which I am privileged to work with others.

BUBBLEGUM, RIP

{January 7, 2010}

I don't know what it was about those words or about how he said them but we connected deeply in that very brief moment. He told me with that comment that he appreciated my being there for him, for loving him through a tough ordeal and for helping us to move on.

We are not "pet people." We are "kid people." And, whenever our kids ask us, "Can we get a dog?" I like to say, "As soon as you come up with the $15,000 to fence our property, yes, we can get a dog." But, I don't really mean it. Pets, as a general rule, just aren't our thing.

As you may know, however, children are persistent. And, in the face of this persistence from our now 10-year-old son, we decided a couple of years ago to become pet people, at least in a very small way. We bought a rat, and our son named her Ginger, as in the Gingerbread Man from Shrek. We soon learned that rats are social animals, and unless you're going to be playing with your rat all the time, it's important for her to have a companion.

Bubblegum joined our clan about six months after Ginger. She soon proved herself an annoying cage-mate for her "older sister," but settled in and then just proved herself slower, fatter and more susceptible to biting off the end of your finger. That said, we had her and she had us and we were pet people times two.

About a week before Christmas, Bubblegum fell. She landed hard on the concrete as our son was tending to the chore of weekly cage cleaning. To say he was sick about it is an understatement. To say she was OK would be a massive understatement. She most definitely was not OK. We took her to the vet (words I can't believe I'm writing because we aren't "pet people" so certainly we must not be "vet people." Alas.) and learned that while nothing was broken, per se, she clearly had suffered some head trauma and we needed to give her a week or two of serious R&R. I don't exactly know what that means for a "fancy rat," but for us that meant separating her from Ginger, putting her in a smaller, simpler cage so she wouldn't climb and just watching her and hoping she improved.

Immediately after the fall, as we were assessing Bubblegum's condition, I gently but firmly attempted to prepare my son for the worst. I explained that we would not be taking extraordinary measures to help Bubblegum but that we would do what we could and involve the experts at least a little bit, but certainly not too much. He understood, or at least he lied to me very convincingly. That first night we even talked briefly about the possibility of her death, either as the natural result of her fall or perhaps through "putting her to sleep" to end any suffering. We had that discussion through tears. Me, my son, in our kitchen, crying about the possible death of our pet rat, Bubblegum. Oh boy.

Two weeks came and went and she was getting worse. She couldn't do normal "rat stuff" like climb or balance and she definitely wasn't eating or drinking enough. Back to the vet we went. And, of course, I was thinking that three of us were going but that only two of us would be returning home. I was right about that.

The doctor was wonderful. She asked us how Bubblegum was doing. We explained through our tears. She explained her theory about what was wrong. We cried. She explained options: steroids, more watching/waiting, and finally, euthanasia. We cried some more. Obviously her quality of life was gone. Obviously she didn't deserve to live like this. Obviously I wasn't going to spend a bunch of money on a fantasy. That may sound harsh.

Maybe if it was a dog…I don't know.

We made our decision. We left her in the doctor's care. We cried some more. When we got home, I told my son that I would clean out her cage. I figured that the least I could do for him was to honor both him and her by putting things right again, such as I could. He stayed in the car. In the process of my cleaning-up, I retrieved the trashcans from the curb and as I was pulling them back to the side of the house, he hopped out of the car and said, "I'll get those, Dad." I don't know what it was about those words or about how he said it, but we connected deeply in that very brief moment. He told me with that comment that he appreciated my being there for him, for loving him through a tough ordeal and for helping us to move on.

In her death, Bubblegum brought us together. She allowed a father and son to have their first shared experience of loss. An opportunity that is sure to live inside both of us through the years, providing a foundation for the difficult and painful transitions that await us in the future.

WE HAVE TO MEET
PEOPLE WHERE
THEY ARE. NOT AS
WE WISH THEY
WERE OR NEED
THEM TO BE. JUST
AS THEY ARE. THIS
IS THE GREATEST
EXPRESSION
OF LOVE.

GRADUATION DAY

{June 15, 2010}

My daughter graduated from kindergarten today, the first of many commencements to mark her life of learning. In the past I've been a little cynical about things like kindergarten graduations. I think of the line from the 2004 movie *The Incredibles* when Mr. Incredible, incredulous that he has to attend his child's fourth-grade graduation, says, "We keep finding new ways to celebrate mediocrity." It's kindergarten, for goodness sake. One down and a whole bunch more to go.

No such cynicism for me today. Today is a day to celebrate a very special event in the life of a very special girl. Avery is as smart as they come. The problem is, she's not smart in the way the school system needs her to be smart. She doesn't conform to some of the "standard operating procedures" teachers require to effectively manage too-full classrooms. (A kindergarten class in California today has 34 students.) It makes it pretty obvious why a child who strays from the behavioral or academic midline needs the accommodations of a "special day class." Yes, my daughter is "special."

She started having seizures when she was about a year old. Her epilepsy has been successfully controlled with medication for a long time now, but the impact of that early seizure activity has had staying power. The best evidence of it is in her fine motor skills and her emotional immaturity. This is a terribly difficult combination when you are learning how to write, among other things. We believe she knows how to do the work, that the cognitive ability is there. When it comes to executing a task like forming letters, however, it can be painfully frustrating for her, and she makes that clear by either acting out or withdrawing.

In the face of all of this, her progress over the past two years has been remarkable. It is the result of her own very hard work, patient and dedicated teachers and, most significantly, a mother whose advocacy for her daughter is unconditional.

Watching her today, it was clear to me that Avery's learning path is truly going to be her own. There will be both significant challenges and glorious victories. And, if the last few years are any measure, it will be anything but boring.

Thank you, Avery, for putting my cynicism in its place. Thank you for showing me another way to see the world. My pride in your achievement is massive. My hope for your future is abundant. My confidence in your singularity is beyond measure.

THE MYTH OF THE INDIVIDUAL

{July 22, 2010}

...there is nothing I will ever accomplish in my life, at any level or to any degree of significance, that will not require the faithful support, trust and deep generosity of others.

A friend of mine once told me that I'd make a great consultant because of my ability to "detach." I think he meant that while I'm good at helping a group or a team identify and work toward their goals, I'm not really interested in being a team member, allowing me to remain unattached from outcomes and an objective source of perspective and support.

At the time I took it as a compliment because it validated my self-perception. I valued my autonomy, the ability to be (or at least act like) the expert but to do so in my own way, on my own terms. I liked being needed and I valued the ability to leave when I was done. Mostly I liked that this model kept things very clean. No attachments and no mess.

Today, I don't see it as a compliment. What I believe is that my friend was seeing me accurately and describing what he saw in very generous terms. I believe he saw someone who was on the run: afraid to attach because of what it would demand of me; afraid to be needed because I might not have enough to give; afraid to be part of a team because doing so would require me to care less about myself and more about others; afraid to be about "us" instead of about "me."

The myth of the individual is about thinking I can do more on my own than I can do with others.

The myth of the individual is saying, "I did it by myself" and "Look how great I am," not hearing how these are really hollow pleas for affirmation and recognition.

The myth of the individual is that being separate brings distinction, when it really brings isolation.

The myth of the individual is that others are a means to an end rather than a source of joyful support, encouragement and inspiration.

The myth of the individual is that keeping score of my riches is more fulfilling than making riches possible for others.

The myth of the individual is that I was born and will die alone, as if no one has provided for me along the way; maybe not everything, and maybe not how I would have wanted it, but enough.

The myth of the individual is that by playing it safe I protect against my fear of loss instead of risking the real loss that comes from a life lived in self-imposed exile.

The truth is this: there is nothing I will ever accomplish in my life, at any level or to any degree of significance, that will not require the faithful support, trust and deep generosity of others.

WON'T ASK, WON'T TELL

{October 5, 2010}

I was scared to ask for what I needed for fear of revealing myself as incompetent.

My stepfather was a physician. He was also an amateur racecar driver. Clearly a very smart man, he was also a very quiet man. I would never have known about the racing (which, from my 10-year-old perspective, was WAY more interesting than his being a doctor) except for a few framed photographs that hung over the workbench in the garage. I learned over the years that he was a tinkerer. He liked to work on things, figure things out and fix them if he could. This made him both a good doctor and a good mechanic.

Regrettably, I didn't learn any of these skills from my stepdad between the ages of 10 and 16. By this point he had turned from race cars to golf, a decision that resonates to this day but no more so than on one summer afternoon in 1986.

When my sister and I were in high school and both of driving age, my stepdad bought us a car to share. I wish I could remember exactly what kind but it wasn't much to speak of, an early '80's Datsun hatchback or something like that. We didn't have it for too long because I killed it. I'd like to say that my sister killed it, and it's not like she didn't try to kill it, but I just didn't give her quite enough time. The role of "car killer" fell to me and happened, ironically enough, through my effort to take care of it. It seems that I was mistakenly putting engine oil where the transmission fluid was supposed to go. Not good.

I first learned of this transgression one sunny Saturday afternoon while driving south on Interstate 15 on my way to see a girlfriend. This was a pretty long drive for a young driver (freeways and all!) so I was definitely pumped up with manly awesomeness of the "I have a car and I'm driving it to see my woman" variety. Imagine the surprise to both my vehicle and my awesomeness when the car lurched and died, forcing me to the side of the road. I have no idea how I contacted my girlfriend, but a little while later she and her father came to collect me, shamefaced and beaten as I was.

Today, it's a funny story. At the time, not so much. I remember being scared on the side of the road, obviously concerned about the car and what mom and stepdad (not to mention my sister!) would think and say. And I also remember, in taking care of the car, that I knew that I didn't know what I was doing (let's call it "conscious incompetence"). I was acting in good faith but I didn't have a damn clue about what was under the hood, much less what to do about any of it. And, of course, my stepfather knew everything about it and in providing us with the car he never said a word. Not a word.

Why didn't I ask? Why didn't he offer?

The truth is, I was scared to ask for what I needed for fear of revealing myself as incompetent. As for my stepdad, something prevented him from sharing vital information. Maybe he assumed we knew more than we did. Maybe he assumed we would ask. Whatever the reason, we collaborated in failure.

My son is 10 years old. When the time comes, I'm going to show him where the oil goes. That is, if I can find it myself.

ALL MY FEARS AND FAILURES

{*November 22, 2010*}

The vulnerability of asking to be embraced – to be accepted – just as I am can be overwhelming. I would first have to accept myself, an even more difficult proposition.

I choked up during the opening song at church this morning. Two verses into it and I'm standing there, overwhelmed. I don't know why it hit me so hard, but it stayed with me all day. As only music can do, it burrowed inside me and stole my breath before I knew what hit me. Here's the line that landed the blow:

> *"So take me as you find me, all my fears and failures…"*

It's a simple, powerful request to be accepted, embraced, loved and respected for exactly what I am and exactly how I am. In my spiritual tradition this acceptance is a promise of faith that I have a responsibility to live into. It's waiting for me whether I am willing or able to see it; whether I am willing or able to allow myself the comfort of that embrace.

As overwhelming as that kind of acceptance is, more overwhelming still is the responsibility to offer it to others. That's the message of the song that's hardest to accept. Those "others" are all around me every day; looking and quietly asking for a generosity of acceptance, hopeful that I will see them not for who they are, but for the better self they are trying to be.

And there I am asking them to do the same for me.

CONNECTION CAN HAPPEN IN AN INSTANT. IN THAT UNEXPECTED MOMENT, WHAT WILL WE GIVE?

HAPPY

{June 7, 2013}

I walked out of the house this morning, dog on leash, for my daily dose of exercise only to find a garbage truck broken down in front of our home. We never actually see the garbage man because he usually comes by much earlier and doesn't hang around very long in the conduct of his duties.

As I approached, I noticed him talking to another man from the waste removal company who had arrived in his own vehicle to provide service to the malfunctioning truck.

When my garbage man saw me, he greeted me with one of the warmest, kindest, most sincerely expressed smiles and waves I have ever received. His energy and spirit of connection was overflowing and the generosity of his offering them to me was so significant that I was momentarily overwhelmed.

This happened in an instant. I didn't even break stride and I barely returned the greeting, so crushed was I by his unexpected goodness.

All I knew in that moment is that my garbage man is happy, so much so that he can't help but give it away.

As I walked on I could only ponder what impression I make on people in that moment, that briefest moment, of unexpected interaction. Do they walk away crushed by my goodness? Do they get the best of me? Or do I offer something more calculated, more focused on self-preservation than generosity?

My garbage man is happy. And I am, too. I wonder who knows it.

...SIMPLE AND CONSISTENT CONNECTION, GROUNDED IN EMPATHY AND HUMILITY, IS AS CRUCIAL FOR FATHERS AND SONS AS IT IS FOR LEADERS AND FOLLOWERS. GUESS WHO HAS TO GO FIRST?

CONNECTION

{July 8, 2013}

I am the father of a 13-year-old son and lately it's been a little rough. He is in the early stages of a developmental period that is referred to in psychological circles as the "second individuation." The first "individuation" commonly happens at about five years old when boys work hard to separate from "mommy" and look to dad as the model of all things masculine. This is when dad becomes "superhero" as in, "My dad is faster/stronger/smarter than your dad."

As we all know, this idealization comes to a screeching halt not long after puberty hits. It's a bummer, too, because I really like being idealized. Well, at least compared to "deidealization," another psych term for, you guessed it, the deconstruction of dad as superhero and the reconstruction of dad as moron.

For the record, my son is a beautiful young man: handsome, kind, smart and funny. He's a great athlete, has many friends and seems to be navigating the hormonal roller coaster of puberty with a lot of grace and poise. At least he's doing better than me.

Lately I find myself biting at everything he casts, responding automatically and emotionally rather than from the higher ground of understanding or with any empathy for the reality of the circumstances. I'm not suggesting I should be an automaton or a pushover, but it serves me well to remember that I am his primary target right now because, though he loves me greatly, he has to normalize me if he's going to normalize his own experience, if he's going to separate from his parents well as he formulates and establishes his own identity.

At the beach yesterday, as my son was surfing, my wife and I decided to throw the Frisbee. A few minutes later he joined our game and asked me to throw to him as he dove into the waves. Following a few successful connections – well-timed throws and leaps resulting in thrilling last-minute catches before being pummeled by the waves – it hit me with a blinding flash of the obvious that I have forgotten to emphasize the single greatest opportunity I have to stay "close enough" to my son during this transition: I have forgotten about the power of simple connections.

For many dads and sons, the language of connection is spoken through many literal and repetitive acts of connection. Throwing, catching, hitting and shooting – me to you, you to me, from here to there and so on – are the shared actions through which we have established masculine intimacy and meaningful relationship. As we tossed the Frisbee yesterday, celebrating our hits and laughing off our misses, I remembered that reality and welcomed the simple respite from the biological and psychological forces that are hard at work in reshaping our relationship for the shared joys and struggles yet to come.

A leadership corollary: I have yet to read an employee engagement survey that doesn't include strong statistical and anecdotal data describing the desire for more access to and interaction with senior management and more recognition for contributions to organizational goals. In short, people are repeatedly and consistently asking for more connection; simple, intimate and sincere connection – the corporate equivalent of a game of catch –to demonstrate that leaders see employees as human beings hungry to make a meaningful contribution to something worthy of their best efforts.

It seems to me that simple and consistent connection, grounded in empathy and humility, is as crucial for fathers and sons as it is for leaders and followers. Guess who has to go first?

I AM THE KIND OF PERSON WHO...

{August 19, 2013}

...sharing more of ourselves is a catalyst for others to share more with us and pretty soon we build up a virtuous cycle of shared knowledge that helps to increase trust and deepen relationships?

The Johari Window is a simple and clear model which reminds us that the best way to build trust and meaningful relationships is to share more of ourselves with those we wish to know. Sharing more of ourselves typically works as a catalyst for others to share more with us and pretty soon we build up a virtuous cycle of shared knowledge that helps to increase trust and deepen relationships. I have recited this same truism a thousand times. However, as many times as I make this case in front of audiences, teams or coaching clients, I inevitably get a somewhat strained (to put it lightly) response:

1. "You expect me to tell people about myself?"

2. "How much do I have to share?"

3. "You expect me to ask my employees about themselves?"

4. "How much do I have to know?" (An important subtext of this question is another unspoken question, "What if I don't want to know/I don't care?")

My answers:

1. "Yes, I do expect that."

2. "I have no idea how much you should share. Use your common sense."

3. "Yes, I do expect that."

4. "You need to know as much as necessary to make it feel like a real relationship and not some fabrication intended to manipulate others into doing what you want."

And that's where this becomes a leadership discussion. If you are a leader, your job is to learn about and care about your people and to help them — based on what you know about who they are and what the organization needs — to make as big and meaningful a contribution as possible to the enterprise. If you can't do that or if you aren't even willing to try, you absolutely have no right calling yourself a leader.

That said, if you're up for a little (simple and easy) professional relationship-building exercise suitable for either an individual or a team setting, try this:

Have everyone privately write down 10 responses to the following statement:

"I am the kind of person who..."

Get together and share your responses. Using flip chart paper is best because then you can also see what they wrote as they take you through it, but just reading it to one another will work just fine.

You can't respond to the statement 10 times without revealing something personal/interesting/curious/fun/enlightening about yourself. Don't overthink it; it's just what happens. Then you'll be off and running with newfound information about your colleagues and peers and, if you are at all intrepid and even slightly curious, you'll turn that into a relationship-building gold mine.

Give it a try.

YOUR ATTENTION

{October 29, 2013}

"All that we are concerned with is turning your attention to the real things outside."

– John C. Merriam

The Yavapai Point Geology Museum is located along the South Rim of the Grand Canyon at a point selected to give the visitor the most comprehensive visual understanding of the canyon's ancient geological lineage.

Through its thorough and thoughtful descriptions and exhibits, it offers a compelling reminder of how necessary it is to ground ourselves in a fundamental understanding of a place if we are to appreciate its depth and meaning. It takes pains to remind us that its purpose is to equip us to go out and encounter the canyon directly, not to claim our attention, just to borrow it for a little while.

The internal work we do – the work of starting within – we do not for the purpose of self-satisfaction or self-congratulation. We do it because it allows us to meet the world exactly as it is with greater capacity, composure and confidence.

We do it because we recognize that we are called to both live and lead at a higher level. There is a yearning from those working within the complex systems we have created to radically alter their experience of them and to perhaps change them entirely.

Will we respond to that yearning? Will we choose to find new paths out of old stuck places? Will we choose to lead, first ourselves and then, better equipped for having done our own work, turn our attention to those people, those "real things" outside?

THE PERSON IN FRONT OF YOU RIGHT NOW IS THE MOST IMPORTANT PERSON IN THE WORLD

{June 6, 2014}

What he requires to be effective as a communicator is the intimacy, connection and consideration of a thoughtful face-to-face interaction.

At a speaking engagement recently, I met a man who was almost completely deaf. He told me that the most important leadership quality is the ability to listen. Coming from anyone else, this would seem to be an obvious statement, almost a cliché. For him, it was not.

He expressed to me that, even with his hearing impairment, he understands people very well when he is speaking to them face-to-face and one-on-one. Once a conversation grows to include even one additional person, however, he can understand only about 15% of what's being said. (I wonder if those of us with "full" hearing do much better?)

As I was talking with him I noticed myself paying very careful attention to how I expressed myself. I took greater care to articulate my words. I took greater care to check for understanding. I became more thoughtful in listening to his responses and questions because I didn't want to miss anything, because I wanted him to know that I was fully present.

I did that with him because it was obvious that I needed to. I did that because without intention, attention and focus from both of us, our interaction would not be successful. What would happen if I brought that same consideration to every conversation? What would happen if we all did?

He went on to tell me that he had recently declined an invitation to assume a leadership role in an organization he supported because he couldn't imagine how a person with a hearing impairment so severe could effectively lead others. My heart sank.

I told him that any organization would be fortunate to experience his leadership; to learn how to truly listen to one another through his example and necessity. I don't think I changed his mind. What he requires to be effective as a communicator is the intimacy, connection and consideration of a thoughtful face-to-face interaction. Sadly, wise to the world as he is, he knows that what he needs is too prohibitive, too time-intensive, too slow. And so he opts out.

I understand completely why, under the circumstances, he doesn't want to lead.

What he doesn't know, however, is that, through his influence on me, he already has.

HOW TO BUILD CAPABILITY BEFORE YOU NEED IT

{August 18, 2014}

...these are the direct and specific actions I believe leaders must take if they are to be successful in building capability for the future.

I expressed some strong opinions recently about the need for leaders to challenge their organizational practices, especially during periods of great success. Since we know that nothing lasts forever, a healthy, necessary and realistic point of view for leaders to take is that whatever is working right now will not necessarily work next year. Rationally, we all get that. Emotionally, however, we are loath to question ourselves when things are going well, as if we might somehow "jinx" our good fortune. Harry Potter taught an entire world of wizards that not only was it ok to "speak his name" (Voldemort, that is), but it was actually necessary to do so to have any chance of defeating him.

A reader let me know he thought my writing was short on specifics and challenged me to provide some suggestions for this dilemma. Nothing here is new. And yet almost all of it remains unpracticed by most organizational leaders in most organizational settings.

To be clear, these are the direct and specific actions I believe leaders must take if they are to be successful in building capability for the future. I have divided the list into three categories: ***Developmental, Strategic and Cautionary.***

DEVELOPMENTAL

1. Go to therapy. Don't walk, run. Since many leaders are narcissists and all leaders have narcissistic qualities, they are more fragile than they appear to be. (Both Michael Maccoby and Manfred Kets de Vries have written extensively and powerfully on the subject.) When they are wounded by criticism and questioning of their leadership, they often don't heal very quickly and may actually go to great lengths to even the score. As you know, it can get pretty ugly. And, since everything else I am about to advocate involves building infrastructure to question the system, leaders need to build a tough and thoughtful resilience to bear it well. They need to learn not to take every new idea for improvement as an indictment of their leadership but rather as an invitation to keep getting better. For that to happen, those narcissistic wounds are better worked out in the therapist's office than in the boardroom.

2. Send all key leaders to therapy. For all of the reasons stated above.

3. Or at least provide them with highly skilled coaching support. A great coaching relationship can and often does feel "therapeutic" (one senior leader I worked with referred to it as "couching"). The key is to have a safe, trustworthy partner to work through the holistic challenges of work, home and health, all necessary subjects for an effective executive to discuss and work on regularly.

4. Be more human than otherwise. That is to say, thoughtfully reveal your vulnerability, things you're working on, challenges you face. Items #1-3 will be very helpful in equipping you to do this. When you become accessible to your team as a human being, you increase your power by strengthening your connections. Those connections become the lifeline for communication. And communication is at the heart of learning how to get better.

5. Treat people like adults. Respect them enough to be transparent about what's going on. Be clear about what you need. Expect them to do the same for you. You're not their mom or dad. You don't have to protect them from the truth. You do need to give them a chance to rise to the occasion. If they can't or don't, you'll have the information you need to support them in their own development or help them to make a dignified exit.

STRATEGIC

6. *Make every leader accountable for a meaningful annual report of what needs to change in his or her function in the coming year.* There is always something to improve. Always. Building in this kind of evaluative, reflective process expands our capacity for having hard discussions and normalizes the process of doing so. This is to be done in open dialogue with the whole team, starting with the people who are actually doing the work each day. A simple question for them: If you could change one thing that would allow you to be more effective in fulfilling your job responsibility, what would it be? (Note: if you don't get useful answers the first time around, it's probably because they don't trust you enough to be honest. Earn their trust by keeping at it in a sincere and authentic way. If that's hard for you, see item #1.)

7. *Determine how you will change first.* No meaningful change happens until the leader decides to change. Figure out what change in your behavior will help bring about the larger change initiative and get busy. "Be the change you want to see in the world" is not an invitation, but an admonition.

8. *Hold pre- and postmortem meetings for every project.* In the pre-meeting, ask as many people as possible what they think could go wrong. Learn to anticipate the bumps and get your team ready to respond. The postmortem is more of a no-brainer but usually overlooked because we're already off to the next thing. Even a couple of simple questions – again, asked of all involved – will build openness and a greater capacity for learning: What worked? What didn't? What did you learn about yourself and our team?

9. *Expect leaders to coach their teams and teach them how to do so.*
Here's a fine job description for a key leader: Spend time everyday understanding the business and how all the pieces fit together (educate your team about same). Critically consider what's working and what's not in your function and engage your team in frequent dialogue about same. Make plans for improvement by seeking as much perspective as possible. Assign responsibilities to follow through on plans. Provide coaching support and resources to ensure success. Recognize and celebrate publicly and tangibly. This is a "talking, engaging, coaching, critical thinking, relationship" job. It is not a "protect, defend, isolate, manipulate, scheme and otherwise preserve hierarchical hegemony" job.

CAUTIONARY

10. *Don't just pretend to do any of the above.* Up to now, I've offered suggestions on what to "do." Here's my first and only "don't do": Any inauthentic attempt at any of the above will be sniffed out immediately and seen for the manipulative tactic that it is. You've got to mean it or don't even bother. Good people will leave and you will be surrounded by scared people all too willing to tell you that you're great and that what "we're doing" is just right and will certainly last forever. Until it doesn't and you end up in therapy anyway.

I WILL FOLLOW YOU

{September 16, 2014}

You model and expect an ongoing conversation between the
safety of the known and the edges of possibility.

I will follow you because you have a clear and emotionally compelling vision for the future. You want to create meaning because it binds us
together in a cause worth fighting for. That's what I want, too.

I will follow you because you are secure enough – courageous enough
– to lead from your heart. You know that relationship is built from vulnerability, not certainty. Your strength is in your deep understanding that
our connection will matter more than your competence when we hit the
toughest obstacles on our path.

I will follow you because you see every challenge as an opportunity to
learn. You know that learning is the only way to navigate complexity and
change. You model and expect an ongoing conversation between the safety
of the known and the edges of possibility.

Meaning. Connection. Learning.

Yes, I will follow you.

EXPLANATIONS
EXIST; THEY HAVE
EXISTED FOR ALL
TIME; THERE IS
ALWAYS A WELL-
KNOWN SOLUTION
TO EVERY HUMAN
PROBLEM – NEAT,
PLAUSIBLE, AND
WRONG.

– H.L. Mencken

THE MESSY HUMAN REAL THING

{February 16, 2015}

The journey from the Age of Machines to the Age of Meaning is proving to be a bumpy one. It's telling, and not at all surprising, that the more complicated and pervasive technology becomes, the more people seem to want to get out of the "cloud" and back on the ground. Our collective cognitive dissonance suggests that we believe we can get the meaning and connection we seek if only our technology continues to offer better, faster means of doing so. As that dissonance festers, our only choice is to resolve it by either letting go of our need for authentic connection or reconsidering the role and purpose of technology. That's not much of a choice.

In the Age of Machines, people are treated like machines in order to build machines. In the Age of Meaning, people are treated like people who are brought together by the common cause of creating something of value, machine or otherwise. There is a shared human need to connect to something larger than ourselves; while technological solutions can provide tools to aid that connection, to assist in that creation, it's time to stop confusing that assistance with being an end unto itself. It is, in fact, a terrible substitute for the real thing.

But the real thing – the messy human real thing – is precisely why we keep turning to technology. The clean landscape of ones and zeros tempts us to believe we can manufacture a more Disney-like version of the human experience. For too long we've been trying to outsmart ourselves and it's time to get real about that. Despite our clever ability to build an even better mousetrap, at some point we must learn that the path to freedom demands a humble reckoning with what has been denied: each heart's deep longing to be seen, heard and understood.

When the organization becomes a place where that can be expressed freely, openly, and with a strategic understanding of its relevance to the bottom line, the Age of Meaning will have arrived.

RIGHT AND LEFT

{February 23, 2015}

When we are finally able, first in ourselves, to forge a faithful marriage of right and left, we will have done something extraordinary: we will have become fully human for the first time.

We need them both. And we need the courage to say so.

Let the right represent the preservation of the system. Let the left represent the idealism necessary to pursue possibility in the face of the unknown.

We need leaders who will dispel the temptation to remain committed to the singular, limiting notions of control and rationality.

We need leaders who are willing to tap into the resources of the heart. The rough-around-the-edges, uncertain and vulnerable qualities of the heart. This requires the deep courage to say, "I don't know," followed by an unequivocal, "But I'm willing to learn whatever it takes to help us figure it out."

I can't imagine anything more inspirational, more connective, and more human.

When we are finally able, first in ourselves, to forge a faithful marriage of right and left, we will have done something extraordinary: we will have become fully human for the first time.

THE HUNGER FOR
CONNECTION IS SO
GREAT, AND THE
EASE OF ACCESS
SO HIGH THAT
EXPECTATIONS HAVE
SKYROCKETED.

ALWAYS ON

{February 25, 2015}

There is an Internet meme of Abraham Maslow's "Hierarchy of Needs" modified to show Wi-Fi as the base or most fundamental level of human need, before food, clothing and shelter. While this is hilarious (to me, anyway), it's also redundant to what appears further up the ladder. Access to Wi-Fi as a fundamental human need is only restating that access to connection – see "Belonging - Love" on the middle tier – is essential.

What I am not clear on, and what I think very few people are clear on since we are still in the early adolescence of our use and understanding of these technologies, is how much of the "old school" qualities of connection these "new school" resources can actually provide. If only using my own behavior as an example, I notice a shadow over my need to be always "on." Because I don't know what might be coming, or what I might find, I inhabit my phone and my email with a sort of anticipatory anxiety of need fulfillment. I have learned that I am not unique in this. There are different flavors and varieties, of course, but the hunger for connection is so great and the ease of access so high that expectations have skyrocketed. When I am disappointed that the only things that have arrived in my inbox overnight are the same old subscriptions, it is a sure sign that I am taking for granted the connections – again, the belonging and love –that exist for me in my very household!

Do I assume that I know the capability of those relationships to fulfill my needs for connection? Do I allow the mystery and myth of some unforeseen validation to distract me from that which exists in the morning greeting of my daughter or the tail-wagging enthusiasm of our dog? Apparently so.

The Internet, email, texting, none of it came with a guidebook for how it can help to enhance human relationships. We have to figure that part out on our own. As for my steep learning curve, I must admit that (A) I am in deep and continuous need of validation, connection, support and love, and (B) I have a mountain of it right in front of me.

To my great benefit and continuing astonishment, it is always "on."

WORDS TO LEAD BY

{March 2, 2015}

This partial list reminds me just how difficult true leadership really is. It is hard work and not for the timid, requiring deep reserves, great strength, and the ability to let go. The cost is high, the rewards are extraordinary.

Clarity: you know what you are trying to accomplish at personal, team and organizational levels. You've put in the time to get clear.

Meaning: you share your vision liberally because you know that everyone wants to contribute to something larger than him- or herself. The strength of your vision makes others want to declare their own.

Creativity: you are faithful to the belief that everyone is creative but that you can only access that creativity in a safe, supportive, productive and energized environment. These are nonnegotiable conditions.

Energy: you take care of yourself because your output is always the high-water mark for the team, and perhaps the organization. No one is more enthusiastic, determined, focused, or emotionally available than you.

Capacity: you take on all of the change, complexity, uncertainty and ambiguity. Everyone is looking to you for what to do next. You will need a bigger bucket.

Connection: you demonstrate an hour-to-hour and day-to-day quality of concern and affection for every team member. It is sincere and it comes from your heartfelt belief that human relationship is the cornerstone of the best kind of productivity.

Vulnerability: you openly discuss what's working and what's not about yourself, the team and the organization.

Thank you: you habitually and authentically express gratitude in a clear and straightforward way because you know it is more valuable, and more sought after, than any "employee recognition event" will ever be.

Celebration: you make team events a priority –and make them fun, meaningful and energized – and you use them to highlight the great things your team has done.

Candor: you move toward the hard stuff. You do it from a place of empathy, consideration and respect and you never avoid the real conversation.

Learning: you live from a beginner's mindset. You are always learning.

Space: you hire the best people you can find, set the parameters for their work, are redundant about your values (the rules of the road), and then you let them go.

Help: you ask for it. You don't have all the answers. Anyone who thinks you should is stuck in an old model that is literally falling apart all around them.

This partial list reminds me just how difficult true leadership really is. It is hard work and not for the timid, requiring deep reserves, great strength, and the ability to let go. The cost is high, the rewards are extraordinary.

Pick a word this week and see what you can do to make it come alive for you and your team. Just one word…and see what happens.

THE BEST THEY CAN

{March 4, 2015}

When everyone around you seems to be reading from a different script – and getting different results – it can wear after a while. It did with me.

Everything I read about coaching eight-year-olds in basketball says that the emphasis needs to be on having fun. Those who take the time to write about such things emphasize that a coach's first and most important job at this level is to help the kids discover their athleticism by making it so much fun that they fall in love with it and can't wait to come back, next practice, next season, et cetera. No one suggests teaching the crossover dribble or the fade-away jump shot.

When my nine-year-old daughter decided she wanted to play a second season of recreational basketball, I responded enthusiastically. Her first season was a steep learning curve – fun, but steep – and I hadn't been sure how she would feel about giving it another try. Flushed with excitement, I made a commitment to her that I would be an assistant coach for her team. I had noticed the year before that her coach could have benefited from some help and I regretted not having stepped up to support him. Not so this year. I was ready to pitch in.

What veteran parents of recreational sports will tell you, about which I was impressively naive, is that there is rarely, if ever, such a thing as an "assistant coach" at this level. The parks and rec folks just need coaches, period. When you offer to be an assistant, it's only a matter of time until you're handed the whistle and clipboard and given a battlefield promotion. I was no exception. Making lemonade from the lemons I hadn't wanted to pick, I invited my son to help me out and figured that I could not only have an experience coaching my daughter, but also the camaraderie of working alongside him.

Consulting my online coaching resources, I mapped out a plan that emphasized fun – lots of running around, lots of games, lots of silliness. Since my own technical basketball skills are limited, I went with my strength and gave the girls as much positive energy and enthusiasm as I could muster. From the very beginning, our coaching approach was a big hit. Thanks to many great suggestions, the girls laughed their way through drills that were cleverly designed to be the building blocks of their athletic development.

I loved basketball as a kid. I played in leagues, with my buddies, or just by myself in the front yard. I would stay outside well after dark, shooting free throws for as long as it took to make ten in a row. Reclaiming this childhood passion, pairing it with my aptitude for motivation and inspiration, and then channeling the combination to my daughter's team was deeply gratifying – until the games started. We didn't win one.

I'm not sure what the formula is for putting teams together for recreational leagues, but it became evident with each team we faced that we were always going to be smaller, younger and less experienced. While this could sound like an excuse or even sour grapes, it was just the fact of the matter. As the losses piled up I began to question my strategy. I began to reconsider whether or not my focus on learning the fundamentals through fun, energy and enthusiasm was most important after all. I found myself reverting back to well-developed feelings of competitiveness and intensity, exasperation, and frustration. When everyone around you seems to be reading from a different script – and getting different results – it can wear after a while. It wore on me. As best I could, I kept all of that to myself for the one reason that mattered most: my players didn't care. The fun strategy was working for them just fine. Since most of these girls were new to basketball, they were too concerned with just being on the court to really care about winning or losing; they just wanted to play.

After our sixth or seventh game, a grandmother of one of the players came up to me and said, "Those girls are just doing the very best they can. There's nothing more you can ask than that."

Every week they got better. Every week they got pushed around a little less and asserted themselves a little more. Every week one of them would have an "aha" moment right in the middle of the game. Every week something would "click" and they would understand what could be possible, if only for a moment. The pride in their smiles was priceless.

I will never again doubt the multiplying effect of energy and enthusiasm. They are infectious and vital to learning.

And it's worth remembering that most of the time, most people are doing the very best they can.

YOU DO KNOW, DON'T YOU, THAT THE PEOPLE YOU ARE MOST THREATENED BY ARE INVARIABLY JUST LIKE YOU?

– Richard Rohr

OTHERS

{March 6, 2015}

I met a friend near the beach yesterday afternoon. We planned to sit and have some conversation, opting not for the coffee shop but for an ocean view. It was low tide and the beach was expansive, endless flat sand stretching away in either direction.

My friend suggested we take advantage of the tide and stretch our legs. Normally, that's an easy "yes," but I hesitated in light of the fact that I was dressed for "business" – button-down shirt, slacks, dress shoes – having come directly from other meetings.

But the beach was calling and it is surely seemed some kind of sin to ignore it, so we did not. I quickly and awkwardly transformed from "business guy" to "business guy who just decided to take a walk on the beach." Dress shoes off, socks stuffed inside, pants rolled up and very white feet exposed to sun and sand, we set off. I was the fish out of water. But only to me.

I have always had a complicated relationship with relationships. Part of it – a healthier part than I may be able to admit – is due to the fact that when I am surrounded by talented people – smart, funny, accomplished – I often choose to allow their qualities to serve as a measuring stick to which I inevitably am not equal. I would like to be one who celebrates others more freely, reveling in their achievements without it having to have something to do with me, good or bad. Sometimes I am able to do this, sometimes not. When I operate from my lower self, I know it is because I haven't met my own standard and I can't tolerate being reminded of it with the example of others' good work. The easy remedy is to reject and isolate.

But I can't go it alone. I need others and knowing the depth of that need creates a vulnerability that can be hard to take. Others – those most important others – can build us up, make us stronger, accept our awkwardness. Others reflect back to us with precision the truth of who we are. Sometimes, like the glare off of a sparkling ocean, it is impossible to see it without squinting and turning away. It can be hard to look at ourselves.

As I keep learning how to walk in the world, the more I am able to see and understand the complications and possibilities embedded in understanding the self, others, and the new entity that is formed when they come together. It is awkward at times, sort of like a man in business attire casually walking the coastline, but getting your feet wet always is.

NOW. HERE. THIS

{April 10, 2015}

What you can do is decide in this moment, at this place and with these people, that you will become as clear as possible about a few essential things.

Every day – and I mean every day – I spend some time thinking about and feeling my emotions related to the following:

1. Some event or person in my past that hurt me or that I perceive as having hurt me.

2. Concern/anxiety about the future. Will there be enough? Will I be able to provide? Will I have the courage to do what I most want? Et cetera, ad nauseam.

3. What I am doing right now that excites and energizes me, the contribution I am making, the purpose I am living into, the possibility I am fulfilling, the lives I am changing, starting with my own.

A good day is one in which #1 and #2 are kept to a minimum and #3 ascends with vigor. A bad day is when I let the past and/or the future determine the quality of the present. And, more importantly, my presence.

Replaying the difficulties of the past – especially by casting oneself as a victim of circumstance – as if doing so will yield a different outcome, only robs you of the opportunity to create something new in the present.

Anxiously anticipating the future – especially through some story about insufficiency or inadequacy – when all you can control is your own behavior and your own choices, is energy lost to fear of the unknown.

There is nothing you can do to change the past. There is nothing you can do to predict the future.

What you can do is decide in this moment, at this place, and with these people that you will become as clear as possible about a few essential things:

Who you are.

Where you are going.

The next step you can take.

And how much you are willing to love and serve the person in front of you right now

WHY DO YOU TALK TO EMPLOYEES?

{June 25, 2015}

Be careful what you say. Someone might just memorize it and apply it for the next 30 years.

According to a participant in a class I led recently, there are three reasons to talk to employees:

1. They are not getting their job done.

2. They are preventing others from getting their job done.

3. They broke the rules.

The participant shared that they picked up this rule of thumb in a management training class they took over 30 years ago. This was not shared in a "Can you believe they said that?" kind of way, but was brought up in a "Here's something I learned a long time ago and still rely on today" kind of way.

I have two thoughts about this:

1. Thirty years later, we need a new list.

2. Be careful what you say. Someone might just memorize and apply it for the next 30 years.

Here's what I believe is a more valid – though only partial – list of reasons to talk to your employees:

1. You like them.

2. You're interested in them.

3. You want the best for them.

4. You're excited to work together.

5. You want to learn from them.

6. You want to teach them.

7. You want to help them.

8. You want to challenge them.

9. You want to encourage them.

10. You want to console them.

11. You believe that connection is essential for impact.

12. You believe that relationship is the source of meaning.

13. You are always eager for a reality check.

14. You believe that "we" are smarter than "me."

15. You believe that they are indispensable to your success.

16. It would be no fun without them.

17. They make you better.

18. Et cetera...

What's on your old list? What will be on your new one?

Slowly, slowly, slowly the tide is turning. It is turning. We have to believe that.

More importantly, we have to act as if we believe it

GOOD ENOUGH

{August 12, 2015}

The "good-enough" mother...creates the conditions for differentiation and independence and problem-solving skills and resilience.

The following passage is from an article by Jennifer Kunst in which she provides a compelling interpretation of Donald W. Winnicott's concept of the "good-enough mother." As you read it, I invite you to do so in a way that allows it to speak to the identity with which you most associate, i.e., as needed, replace "mother" with father, boss, leader, teacher, etc.

"What I like about Winnicott's picture of the good-enough mother is that she is a three-dimensional human being. She is a mother under pressure and strain. She is full of ambivalence about being a mother. She is both selfless and self-interested. She turns toward her child and turns away from him. She is capable of great dedication yet she is also prone to resentment. Winnicott even dares to say that the good-enough mother loves her child but also has room to hate him. She is not boundless. She is real."

I cannot read this without being flooded with empathy for all of us who struggle with the pressure to be certain, to be right, to be perfect. We would be far better off if we were able to collectively let go of the myths that keep us small in favor of a more accurate accounting of the common humanity that serves to enlarge and enliven us.

According to Winnicott's concept, "The good-enough mother...starts off with an almost complete adaptation to her infant's needs, and as time proceeds she adapts less and less completely, gradually, according to the infant's growing ability to deal with her failure."

The "good-enough" mother creates enough distance from her child, thoughtfully and over time, to allow the child to find its own way. By doing so, she creates the conditions for differentiation and independence and problem-solving skills and resilience. She creates the conditions in which her child can learn how to be among those who thrive in the face of uncertainty, making meaningful contributions to society squarely in the face of the unknown.

It must be for this reason that James Michener once wrote: "I have recently decided that the constructive work of the world is done by an appallingly small percentage of the population....Those men and women who do have the energy to form new constructs and new ways to implement them must do the work of many. I believe it to be an honorable aspiration to want to be among the creators."

As a mother, father, boss, leader or teacher, you have acted on your aspiration to be "among the creators" and you are striving to have lasting impact in the face of challenges and changes too numerous to mention. Your contribution to those you serve, then, will best be measured by the ability you cultivate in them to stand in the midst of uncertainty on their own two feet. Propping them up or protecting them from failure only serves to ensure that they will not be among those who do the "constructive work of the world."

"Good enough" is much more than good enough. It is how, as Abraham Lincoln said, "We shall nobly save...the last best hope of earth."

Author's note: the following four posts were written at quarterly intervals throughout my "100 Days of Connection" project during the summer of 2015.

You can view the photos from the completed project at:
http://issuu.com/davidberry77/docs/100_days_of_connection/1

CONNECTION: 25 DAYS

{June 27, 2015}

...in connection I find comfort, strength, purpose, love and assurance. I also sense a deep vulnerability that it will not last.

Inspired by the 100 Day Project at Yale University, I decided, 25 days ago, to start my own "100 Day" creative discipline. The assignment is simple: choose a theme or focus area and for the next 100 days document/create/design something relevant to that theme.

I chose the theme of "connection" and decided to explore it through photography. That was my first impulse and my only guideline: connection explored visually. To enhance my accountability for the project, I decided to share each day's photo on both Facebook and Twitter, helping me to create both a track record and an expectation of continuation.

Connection has been a sharp edge for me for as long as I can remember. Last month, as I was working on a section of my book – a collection of blog posts organized under the themes of "understanding," "connection," and "exploration" – I found myself struggling to articulate what I wanted to say about the middle category. I came up against feelings of inadequacy and immaturity relative to my ability and willingness to connect and to connect well. I felt a little silly as I attempted to "author" something about a subject long so difficult for me to understand.

The simplest way to explain it is that, in connection, I find comfort, strength, purpose, love and assurance. I also sense a deep vulnerability and fear that it will not last – that I will have to feel the pain of its loss – and I do what I can to make sure that I don't.

I believed that a daily discipline that challenged me to look for connection, think about it, notice it and document it might be just the way to continue to normalize some of those uncomfortable feelings and open me up to some new ways of experiencing one of, if not the greatest, joys of life: being in meaningful relationship with other people.

Here at the 25-day mark, I'll give you a brief description of one specific day to help explain how this experience is shifting my attention and heightening my attunement to connection. On Day 16 – June 17th – I completely forgot to take or post a photo. When I realized this at 7:00 a.m. the next day, I was angry at myself for breaking the chain so soon. My posting that day simply said, "Forgot." When a few people "liked" that post, I was humbled by their recognition of my very human mistake and what I interpreted as their appreciation for my honesty about it. I was just so frustrated that I let connection – and my project – slip my mind until I remembered that June 17th had been a tough day for me. Creatively, I felt stymied, not getting the results in my writing that I was looking for. When that frustration mounts I tend to go "inside," to lock up, disassociate and become critical. I disconnect. No wonder that I missed a day. Connection was not present for me because I wasn't available for it.

CONNECTION: 50 DAYS

{July 23, 2015}

Tell me to what you pay attention and I will tell you who you are.

— *José Ortega y Gassett*

We cannot script our lives. We can only discover them day by day and, in our reflections, learn how our intentions have formed the narrative of our experience. Without intention, we wander, puzzled in our backward glances at the randomness of it all, feeling adrift in the present and concerned about the future. With intention, we learn to pay attention, discovering how our hopes complement life's unfolding, sometimes in ways we want, more often in ways we need.

Had I known when I started this project that the midpoint would coincide with my daughter's tenth birthday, I would have dismissed it as coincidental. From the perspective of the halfway mark, however, I cannot help but see it as an essential indicator. The significance of her birth and growth into such an extraordinary young person and the opportunity to celebrate it in the middle of summer – a time of such energy and emergence – is at the heart of what this experience is trying to teach me: connection is always right here.

It is so easy, so tempting, to look beyond what is closest and most personal as if it couldn't possibly satisfy my heart's desire. But I do that, we all do at times, because connecting with what is nearest also brings the greatest risk of loss. If I simply open my arms to who is before me, a young girl who loves her daddy, I am both overwhelmed by joy and stung by the letting go. Even so, would I dare refuse that embrace? Would I go searching for something "more" as if it could even approach the potency of that relationship? There is no need to go looking for what is right before me. There is only a decision to accept it as it is – all of it – or go on pretending that connection and disconnection are not forever intertwined.

As I review the photographs of the last 25 days, I see a shift toward greater intimacy and awareness. I see more family – my beautiful wife, my charming nieces (even a great-niece!), my children – I see friendship, I see my home, the evidence of a day-to-day life. I also see more of myself reflected in the images I have captured. I see the way that I am gradually becoming the thing to which I am paying attention and how, in doing so, the more connection I am creating. As I share this experience with others, they want to help me connect. Curiosity leads to conversation and eventually to stories. Everyone has a connection story. Everyone wants to share, to be heard. My daughter frequently asks me, "Is that for your connections, Daddy?" She is noticing, too.

As I move into the second half of this "project," my intention is a simple one: to start close in, noticing and receiving the connection that is here and now.

It is intoxicating to be an explorer, captivated by the possibility of hidden treasure. An even greater discovery, though, is in learning how to value what we have already found.

CONNECTION: 75 DAYS

{August 17, 2015}

Connection needs a catalyst, a spark. Sometimes, especially with the people closest to us, we have to work for it.

Some days it just happens. I have an experience or an interaction that is so obviously "connective" and, assuming my iPhone is nearby, so easily captured. A lovely watercolor falls out of a book. A game of backgammon is in full swing. An old friend appears unexpectedly. Those days make me feel like the beneficiary of some divine offering.

Some days I know it's coming. We're going to see these friends at an anniversary celebration or those friends at a going-away party. Those days feel like cheating: I wake up knowing that this day is "covered" and I don't have to "worry" about it. Connection is in the bag.

Some days I have to work for it. I have to be on the lookout and if nothing shows up (or more likely, if I have blindly missed lots of opportunities) I have to make it happen myself. This feels off to me, like I'm engineering the moment in service of the project instead of just experiencing my already connected life. What I have discovered though (and the photo here is a great example of it), is that good stuff can happen when you are set on creating connection. I asked my daughter to come and sit with me so her mom could take our picture. It was 9:30 p.m. on a Friday night and I still didn't have my shot for the day. We started goofing around with weird voices and then she said something that cracked us both up. We kept giggling for a minute or two and Mom captured what had become an authentic moment of connection.

That moment made something concrete for me in a way that I wasn't expecting: connection isn't always pure and organic. It doesn't just "happen" and we can't expect it to. Connection needs a catalyst, a spark. Sometimes, especially with the people closest to us, we have to work for it. Sometimes, even when our vulnerability tells us it is awkward or forced, connection can transform a moment into something altogether new, something for us to savor.

SMALL MOVES: 100 DAYS OF CONNECTION

{September 13, 2015}

What is familiar is not understood precisely because it is familiar.

– G. W. F. Hegel

There is a powerful moment at the beginning of the movie Contact (1997) when young Ellie is calling out on her shortwave radio, trying to find someone, anyone, who might be listening on the same frequency. As her frustration grows, her dad implores her, "Small moves, Ellie. Small moves."

Finally, someone answers. A man from Pensacola. Ellie is so startled that she doesn't know what to say.

The movie takes us from this intimate moment between a father and a daughter to a wormhole in deepest space. The story arcs from what is closest and dearest all the way out to an astonishing celestial frontier before curving back to the familiar ground of the here and now. It reminds us that as far as we might travel to find what we are looking for, the things – the people – we most want and need in our lives are usually very close at hand. Connection always requires small moves, and in my experience, those moves consistently lead right back to what we most need to learn.

This is my lesson after 100 days of seeking connection: I have been looking for something that was not lost. Connection is always one small move away; its familiarity is the perfect hiding place.

Ellie is young when her father dies. What becomes her quest – to discover life on other planets – is really a search for a way back to her dad, a

way back to what is familiar and comforting. Is it any surprise that when she does make contact with an "extraterrestrial," it takes the form of her dad, using the known to settle the confusion of the new?

An early, significant loss can make future attachment very hard. It's just so easy to defend against the possibility of experiencing that old pain in a new way. In my experience, it has always been easier for me to either smother another person to get them to reject me or to coolly keep my distance to avoid revealing my vulnerability. Of course, both responses always left me disconnected and alone, reinforcing my belief that connection could only be attained through a perfect alignment of very specific variables. I have since learned that "all or nothing" is rarely a successful approach when it comes to matters of the heart.

I am just slightly wiser after these 100 days. I am more awake to connection's continuous presence and to the deep satisfaction that comes with moving toward it each day. I am more aware of how small moves often feel insufficient in the moment, like breadcrumbs for a starving man. Through sheer redundancy of attention, I also see that there's no other way to do it. Ellie's discovery of a message from outer space eventually comes from years of dedicated listening, one frequency at a time.

At the end of the film, the alien who has taken the form of Ellie's dad says to her:

"You're an interesting species. An interesting mix. You're capable of such beautiful dreams, and such horrible nightmares. You feel so lost, so cut off, so alone, only you're not. See, in all our searching, the only thing we've found that makes the emptiness bearable, is each other."

DEVELOPING YOUR VOICE OF CONNECTION

A well-developed Voice of Connection is how we let others know that we are committed to powerful relationships as a catalyst for meaningful change. It's how we articulate our belief that we can't "go it alone" and wouldn't want to anyway because doing so is not nearly as much fun. It's how we demonstrate our belief that the purpose of relationship is to make everyone successful in the pursuit of something we all care about. It's also how we embrace the vulnerability that comes with trusting others and how we reassure them through our ability to be trusted.

Some practices to consider for bringing the Voice of Connection alive within yourself and those you lead:

- Listen. Be curious. Listen. Ask Questions. Listen. Ask how you can be helpful. (People love this.)

- Share more of yourself. Go beyond the business card and the organizational charts and give people a sense of who you really are. Doing so will create a reciprocity of dialogue that will eventually reveal how people want to be known.

- Make time for unscripted meetings. Invite people in for a chat or simply walk around the workplace, but create some space for informal and improvisational conversation. Enjoy what emerges. (You don't have "other work to do." This is your work.)

– Tell the truth as fast as you can. People are not fragile. They can take it. Whatever needs to be said, as professional adults they deserve the respect of being dealt with candidly and quickly (with care and concern, of course).

– Stay with the emotion. You'll know you've developed more capacity within yourself when you can sit with someone who is freely expressing emotion and not run screaming from the room! Emotional honesty is a gift. The best we can do is to receive it thoughtfully, strive to understand it, and provide enough space for the person to work through it in his or her own way.

– Consider every relationship the most important relationship you have. Practicing relational integrity means consistency in the quality of your interactions. There is no relationship too small or insignificant to not deserve your best effort.

– Be accessible. Be responsive. Not 100% of the time. No one does that. But enough of the time that people appreciate both your dedication to their well-being and your common humanity.

PART III

THE VOICE OF EXPLORATION

ONCE WE BELIEVE
IN OURSELVES,
WE CAN RISK
CURIOSITY, WONDER,
SPONTANEOUS
DELIGHT OR ANY
EXPERIENCE THAT
REVEALS THE
HUMAN SPIRIT.

- E.E. Cummings

INTRODUCTION

The Torrey Pines glider port is a beautiful expanse of grass that slopes gently down to a cliff edge, about 300 hundred feet below which is one of San Diego's most storied beaches. For my 30th birthday, my wife surprised me with the experience of paragliding above that beach and along that extraordinary stretch of coastline. It remains my single best personal example of the difference between "interested" and "involved."

Fees paid and waivers signed, my instructor helped me into a heavy harness that connected to a large wing (and by "wing" I mean kite, a very big kite). As he did so, it occurred to me that somehow my wing had to go from lying loosely on the ground to being rigidly taut with air. There was no motor attached to the harness. In fact, there was no propellant of any kind to get that wing inflated and off the ground. Just the same, it was apparently possible, as I could see more than a dozen people cruising along the coastline directly over my head.

As my instructor clipped himself into our shared harness, positioned behind and slightly above me, I casually asked over my shoulder, "So, how do we get up there?"

"That's the best part," he said. "We walk off the edge of the cliff."

"I'm sorry? We do what?"

"We walk off the edge of the cliff. Lead the way."

With both the exhilaration of fear and a strange calm born of his confidence, I began a very long, short walk to the edge of the cliff.

What I could not see from my vantage point just 50 yards from the edge was the essential relationship between land and sea that makes it such an ideal spot for paragliding. Rushing off of the ocean that day, like most days, was an onshore breeze reliably careening into the face of the cliff on top of which I was standing, harnessed and ready to go. When the wind hit that wall, there was only one place for it to go: straight up.

As we came closer to the edge, I felt the drag of the wind behind me as it began to fill and lift my wing. We were still a few yards from the drop-off when it had fully expanded and began to pull us skyward. What a feeling! My favorite memory of it is the profound sense of silence. Combined with the visual beauty of land and sea meeting so dramatically, the expansiveness of that silence helped me rethink my overuse of the word "awesome."

In my "yes" to the instruction to move toward the edge of the cliff, to move toward the unknown, I was rewarded with support that I otherwise could not have seen. Had I stayed further up the slope – interested but uninvolved – I would have had no idea that the force of the wind racing up the cliff face was the key to this entire endeavor. I would have failed to understand that only by going to meet it would I be able to embrace its impact and power.

While the wind was my invisible support system, there were many other visible elements working with me and for me to make my flight possible. I was secured to a harness that held me. The harness attached to a wing whose structure captured the wind. I had an expert instructor whose clear guidance and confidence gave me the security and the assurance I needed to take a walk that would lead to flight. My exploration of the unknown was made possible by the presence of support seen and unseen. The magic happened when the two finally had the chance to meet.

I was not alone in my exploration of that edge. I may have been uncertain due to my lack of experience, but just enough of a "beginner's mindset" and the right resources allowed me to turn the potentially negative energy of fear into an positively energized curiosity. I knew that the pieces were in place for this experience to be successful, and even memorable, but I had to move toward the unknown to find out.

I could not have done so by myself. I could not have done so without saying, "Yes!" to the adventurer in me who is always ready to explore.

On the Move

The crossroads of change demand that we lead with a childlike curiosity as we navigate away from the known to learn what the unknown has to teach us. The Voice of Exploration is the voice of being in the world in anticipation of new learning rather than in the world feeling content that we've discovered all we need to know.

Importantly, this quality of exploration is not based on the abandonment of our known, present experience. Rather, it is focused on expansion and extension. It is a commitment to discovering how, starting from the place that we are, we can learn to make that place even better. Sometimes we may leave things alone, sometimes we may leave them behind, but the heart of the intention is to remain open to the possibility of another way.

This openness to reinvention is made possible by the way the voices of Understanding and Connection build on one another in support of the Voice of Exploration. From a commitment to fluency about ourselves and our relationships, we are strengthened in our intention for learning, equipping ourselves to extend toward exploration and discovery. With careful cultivation, these first two voices get us ready for bigger work.

The effort required to articulate our Voice of Understanding serves to clarify our thinking. It leads us to define personal values that guide decision making and a strong sense of purpose to support our intentions. It helps us frame a realistic picture of our strengths and weaknesses and what they can teach us about how to make our best possible contribution. It leads to greater awareness of our aspirations, which allows us to ask for the right kind of help.

From individual clarity comes the possibility of building even more effective relationships. The Voice of Connection creates the conditions for us to find like-minded people who are willing to support our continuous learning and who will count on us to do the same for them. As this network strengthens, we are then able to align ourselves more thoughtfully to the questions that need asking and the risks that need taking. In the face of these unknowns, it makes a big difference to have friends and collaborators we can talk with, walk with and leap with, when necessary.

Understanding and connection serve exploration in the same way that any outdoor experience, even a simple day hike, benefits from thoughtful preparation. By taking the time to equip ourselves with the necessary resources for the experience – and even a few supplies for the unexpected – we boost both our confidence and our capabilities. Our willingness to move forward is a natural extension of the quality and depth of our preparation.

Of course, we also hold the essential understanding that even the best preparation doesn't guarantee our protection. And we still go on the hike – or walk to the edge of the cliff – because we know that we don't have the luxury of sitting on the sideline and hoping for a better set of challenges. We are responsible, as leaders of rapidly changing organizations, for developing a meaningful conversation between our present understanding and the unknowns that hold new possibilities for learning and growing.

This is the power and purpose of the Voice of Exploration.

IT'S OUT ON THE EDGE THAT WE FIND THE WIND TO TAKE US HIGHER.

- Dewitt Jones

EXPLORING THE EDGE

{April 5, 2010}

Last Wednesday afternoon, as I was getting ready for a speaking engagement in the Seattle area, I understood this quote in a new way. Invited there to share my experience and to inspire new kinds of thinking about leadership, learning and change, and just moments away from starting, I noticed a tremendous energy welling up in me. Part nervousness, part exhilaration, part confidence, part humility, it was an energy that could not and would not be ignored. I recognized it is a step toward the future I am creating with every new action that takes me toward the edge rather than back to the middle.

Dewitt Jones is a photographer, long with National Geographic magazine. When I heard him use this quote in the context of human achievement, he was drawing on his experience of watching eagles ride the updraft of wind that races up the face of a cliff. If the eagle doesn't position itself far enough out over the cliff, it can't take advantage of the upward current and reach heights where it can really soar. Now, I don't need to remind you that eagles have specific physical advantages that make hanging out on cliff edges a little less risky for them than for other creatures. Namely, they can fly.

Eagles soar because that's what they are built for. Their purpose in life is to get up nice and high so they can spot and hunt the food they need to feed themselves and their families. I also bet that they really like flying. How could you not? That said, it's hard to imagine them having doubt or fear about the whole enterprise. I'm guessing you wouldn't overhear things like: "Geez, this is awfully high!" or "Hey, uh, tell me again why we have to jump off this rock?" They do it because that's all they know.

As for me, land dweller that I am, I know too much other stuff. I know that I can fall, that the ground is unforgiving and that when I hit it hard I remember it for a very long time. What I too easily forget, however, is what

I have gained by going to my edge and taking that risk of going over. Sure, I've failed and fallen on occasion, but doing so has always been a powerful teacher at exactly the right time. More often, when I've moved toward the edge of experience I've flown just fine, even soared a time or two. And yet these are the moments I so easily forget when faced with another edge, another chance to fly.

Giving my speech last week, I flew again. And this time I will not forget it. I owe it to myself to turn learning into knowledge and that knowledge into motivation for yet another chance to leap into the unknown and ride with humility on all that is there to hold me up.

MEETING HENRY

{June 28, 2010}

I learned that sometimes on the way to what I care about I have to travel on my own. I learned to keep moving forward.

I am a child of the Reagan Revolution. I was 10 years old when the "Great Communicator" entered the White House and I became fascinated with politics, government and American history, especially the presidency itself. As I read more and learned more about the men who had held that office, I found myself increasingly pulled toward Richard Nixon. He was utterly fascinating to me, a tragic character at a tragic time in our country's history, possessing both a brilliant mind and deeply flawed motivations. Nixon and those in his inner circle were redefining the American political landscape in ways they couldn't even imagine.

One morning during the fall of my senior year of high school, I was having breakfast and watching the morning news when I heard that Henry Kissinger was scheduled to speak that day at a conference taking place just 10 minutes from my home. What an opportunity! With absolute certainty I turned to my mom and said, "I'm not going to school this morning. I'm going to hear Henry Kissinger."

I put on a tie, found my way to the conference site and discovered that Dr. Kissinger was the keynote speaker for the annual meeting of the National Radio Broadcasters Association. I walked into the foyer of the ballroom into a sea of adults gathering over coffee and continental breakfast. At that moment my youthful boldness wore off and I was scared. A child impostor, living on the edge, sure to be discovered and tossed out on my ear. And so I did what anyone would do in this situation: I had a Danish. Desperate to fit in, I choked it down and headed toward the ballroom entrance. Once inside, I made what turned out to be both a crucial and fortuitous error: I walked to the far side of the room, leaving myself no escape. I took a seat in the back, hoping to avoid standing out in what was, thankfully, a dimly lit ballroom.

As the proceedings were about to begin, my confidence began to return – I had made it. I survived the gauntlet of the crowd and was poised to hear a very significant man talk about very significant issues. What I didn't count on was that the emcee would stride to the lectern and say: "AS WE DO EVERY YEAR, WE'RE GOING TO KICK OFF OUR MEETING BY HAVING EVERYONE INTRODUCE THEMSELVES AND TELL US WHAT RADIO STATION YOU'RE FROM!" I panicked. There was a very brief moment in which I entertained the idea of introducing myself as "David from WKRP in Cincinnati," but I saw no sense in hastening my doom. As they got started with the introductions, I got the hell out of there, bursting into the foyer only to run smack dab into Dr. Kissinger himself.

More accurately, I ran into Dr. Kissinger's security detail on whose faces I quickly read serious annoyance. As they subdued me (that's a gratuitous word choice but go with me on this), all I could say was, "But I just wanted to meet Dr. Kissinger!" at which point the elder statesman turned around, assessed that I wasn't exactly a threat, and waved me over. I explained that I was a local student interested in hearing him speak. He said a few kind words in that well-known growl of his, signed an autograph for me, and was on his way.

I never did hear him speak. I was too freaked out by that point to go back into the ballroom. But I did get to meet him and that was well beyond what I had imagined over Cheerios and the morning news.

What happened when I got back to school is what I have been thinking about a lot lately. You can imagine my gleeful confidence at being able to report to my classmates what I had done. I was especially excited to go to my government class and share the experience with my teacher, sure that I would be hailed for my boldness in pursuit of a "real" education. This is not what happened. In fact, I remember his reaction as being more annoyed than anything else, annoyed that I had skipped school and annoyed that I was disrupting his class.

He successfully, instantly, drew every breath of wind from my sails. Here I was, engaged in my own learning, taking ownership for it, acting on my passion for the subject matter, only to be met with annoyance and disdain. I was devastated.

In Seth Godin's book, Linchpin, he talks about how the school system, rather than being a catalyst for creative problem solving and leadership skill development, more often than not is just in the way. Sadly, he's right. And I can't help but ask, what of our organizations? In so many ways they just pick up where the schools leave off: Fit in this way. Do it this way. Don't embarrass yourself. Stand out just enough to make a name for yourself but not enough to really share your passion. Don't make us look bad by really caring about your work. Strive for a "met expectations" and be happy with it. You're a cog. That's just the way it is.

Except that it doesn't have to be that way. Not anymore. And, the sooner we figure that out – really figure it out – the better.

I can't help but wonder how things might have been different if that teacher had accurately read my enthusiasm and gone out of his way to nurture, challenge and support it. What new paths would have opened up? What spark would have become a flame?

My experience meeting Dr. Kissinger served a very important purpose in my life. It taught me to move toward what I believe in and to continue to move toward it even when – especially when – it doesn't work out as I had hoped (and it rarely ever does).

WORK ISN'T TO MAKE MONEY. YOU WORK TO JUSTIFY LIFE.

- Marc Chagall

LABOR DAY

{September 6, 2010}

When I was 17 years old I knew exactly what I wanted to do with the rest of my life. I just didn't know that it was possible to apply what came naturally to me to a formal educational or professional pursuit. And so began a 14-year journey to find what it was I was supposed to do, who I was supposed to become and how my part would matter. When I finally landed in my vocation, I was shocked to find that I had known the answer so many years before; that the answer had always been in me, just waiting to be unlocked and reintroduced to the world in a new and more profound way.

Of course, had I not wandered in the desert, searching in vain for the perfect fit; had I not been tested and molded by so many "roads to nowhere," I never would have found the road to somewhere. It was because of the work that was not my work that I was able to find the work that is.

James Michener wrote, and I'm paraphrasing heavily, that until we find our "thing," everything else we do along the way is creative. It's all part of the process of learning who and what we are and how we are meant to use that knowledge in and for the world. And David Whyte, during a presentation about his book, *The Heart Aroused*, said this: "If the path ahead of you is clear, you are on someone else's path."

In other words, your path – the work of your life – is the one with all the obstacles. You have to fight for it, up and over, through and around; clawing, scraping, racing, pushing, pulling. This is how you know it is yours. And, in my experience, while all of that is happening you are deeply gratified by knowing that this fight is your fight, this labor is your labor, this work is meant for you and you alone.

And what a joy it is to find that work! Truly, it is an exceptional feeling to realize that what I do in terms of work is my offering, my contribution.

And with it comes a deep and significant responsibility to fully explore, fully realize, and fully practice that which I am meant to do.

I am grateful this Labor Day to have found my work. More than that, I am grateful to have the permission, support, trust and expectation to fully express it – and myself through it.

"Real generosity toward the future lies in giving all to the present."

- Albert Camus

HOPE, FAITH, LOVE

{September 29, 2010}

Nothing worth doing is completed in our lifetime; therefore
we must be saved by hope. Nothing true or beautiful makes
complete sense in any immediate context of history; therefore
we must be saved by faith. Nothing we do, however virtuous,
can be accomplished alone; therefore, we are saved by love.

– Reinhold Niebuhr

I am wrestling with the idea of creation. I am wrestling with the truth
that any act of creation requires far more than the actual doing of the thing;
far more than a "Eureka!" moment that galvanizes action. I am wrestling
with the realization that creation, as a choice, requires letting go of what I
think it should be to make the space for what it may become.

If I choose to be among the creators, I choose to start something that
cannot be finished; something that may not be understood; something that
will demand an unmatched level of connection to and relationship with
others. If I choose to be among the creators, I must walk a new path rather
than one well worn by the cavalry of what's gone before.

Niebuhr provides us with the framework against which to apply our
creative aspirations. I can almost hear him urging us to let go of completion, sense making, and the trap of perfectionism. He is urging us to trust
that beginning is enough. If it is of deepest meaning to you, begin it. And,
once begun, follow where it leads and call on the help of all who will nurture it to its fullest expression.

Is it worth doing? Is it true and beautiful? Does it invite the contributions of others?

Yes?

Then, with hope, faith, and love in your heart, begin it.

SOMETIMES WE HAVE
TO SQUEEZE THROUGH
A PRETTY TIGHT
SPOT IN ORDER
TO GET TO AN
EXPANSIVENESS WE
COULD NEVER
HAVE IMAGINED.

THROUGH THE EYE OF THE NEEDLE

{October 11, 2010}

Sometimes the smallest openings lead to the largest discoveries. Remember the early scene in the movie Willy Wonka and the Chocolate Factory (1971) when Willy Wonka leads his guests down a hallway that gets smaller and smaller the further along they go? At the very end of the hall is an extremely small door, which, of course, leads into the largest and most spectacular room in the factory.

I found myself in one of those tight spots this morning as my wife and I explored La Jolla Cove on a tandem kayak. With the promise of caves, kelp and sea life awaiting us, we headed out on the water as part of a loosely organized "guided" tour. When we reached the cliff walls that form the cove, we came upon a narrow cave opening that, from the perspective of the open water, looked pretty simple to navigate. What I realized as we entered the gap into the cave is that a good part of the ocean was entering at the same time, and it had a lot more practice than us. We glanced off the right cave wall and surged forward into an open chamber that was pulsing with the unpredictable ebb and flow of the current. It was an effort just to hold the kayak in place, much less to maneuver it around this impressive cavern. Once we got our bearings and had a few moments to take in our surroundings, we were rewarded for our effort. This impressive space, invisible just a few yards offshore, is a monument to the creative collaboration of time, wind and water.

Sometimes we have to squeeze through a pretty tight spot in order to get to an expansiveness we could never have imagined. Sometimes the only thing we can see is a narrow gap beckoning us forward, asking us to believe that with a little faith, a little focus, and a willingness to ride the surge of the forces around us, we will be opened up to something we otherwise never would have seen.

DID YOU PACK THE CHAINS?

{January 1, 2011}

Whatever you've resolved to do, wherever you plan to go, what are you packing for when the road gets rough?

Our biennial trip to celebrate Christmas with my in-laws is a 738-mile, 13.5-hour trek covering almost the entire length of the state of California. Believe it or not, it's a journey we actually look forward to and enjoy. Hitting the road for a trip of this length is always an adventure, holding the promise of unplanned-for experiences and at least one good feast at In-N-Out Burger.

The drive itself is pretty straightforward, much of it through the very flat, very straight Central Valley. There is, however, a fair bit of mountain driving – through the Angeles National Forest in Southern California and a stunning stretch from Redding to Mt. Shasta in the northernmost part of the state. Given the intense weather that rolled down the west coast in late December, I was concerned that our drive through these areas would be challenging, at best, especially if temperatures dipped and snow started to fall.

Having lived nearly my entire life in Southern California, the most interesting driving challenge I've faced is getting stuck in the sand at our favorite beach. So it is always with some trepidation that I consider having to drive on slushy, slippery mountain roads. And it is always reassuring when I locate the dirty and dusty box of tire chains and make them the first thing I pack in the car.

While I don't like the thought of needing those chains and I don't like the idea of actually having to slog around in the cold and muck to put them on, I sure do like knowing that, if the conditions demand it, I have something to turn to so I can keep the journey going. The chains provide traction when there is none. The chains grip the road when the tires can't do it alone. And though I would always rather have clear sailing on calm seas, the fact is that it just doesn't work out that way. Ever.

We've all got journeys to make in the gift of this new year. Whatever you've resolved to do, wherever you plan to go, what are you packing for when the road gets rough? What or who will you turn to on the days when you just can't keep your grip...when you lose traction...when you need a little help?

READY

{February 18, 2013}

There is no such thing as "ready."

If you are feeling "ready" for the big change – the engagement, the move, the child, the job, the conversation, the writing, the experiment, the adventure, the lessons, the commitment, the confrontation – you've probably waited too long.

Courage is at the heart of the Voice of Exploration, a willingness to move into the unknown and by doing so, begin to make it known.

There is no such thing as "ready."

Feel the fear and do it anyway.

It's time to act.

TRAVELLER, THERE
IS NO PATH
THE PATH IS MADE
BY WALKING

STRANGER IN A STRANGE LAND

{March 3, 2013}

Traveller, the path is your tracks
And nothing more.
Traveller, there is no path
The path is made by walking.
By walking you make a path
And turning, you look back
At a way you will never tread again
Traveller, there is no road
Only wakes in the sea.

– Antonio Machado

Being in transition feels weird. It feels incredibly odd to be in a completely new situation professionally and yet have all of my surroundings remain familiar. This is still my house; these are still my children; these are still my clothes; that is still my dog. And yet it all looks and feels so different. Different because that is not still my job. That place I made tracks to and from every day for nearly eight years is no longer my place. Those responsibilities are no longer my responsibilities. Those politics are no longer my politics. Those victories, those losses? Those aspirations and those complexities? None of them are any longer mine.

I feel "out of my body" just a little bit, just enough to feel the disequilibrium of the change. I walked away willingly and with purpose, but that doesn't mean I am clear, confident, or confirmed in my new venture. I am in progress. I am discovering that everything that is the same no longer looks the same because I am seeing it with new eyes, the eyes of someone who must see the world anew if I am to be in it in a new way.

I am in the world in a new way. I am a stranger to it and it to me. It is stunning to me how much possibility there is in a new beginning. That must be why I feel stunned.

I am a traveller on a new path. This is my path. These are my tracks.

Here I go.

Here I come.

AN UNSTRUCTURED LIFE

{March 16, 2013}

I'm a beginner at this, that much is clear. I need to allow myself some space to exist in the unknown, to bounce around a little while I sort it out.

I've been self-employed for two weeks now, so clearly it's time to share my wisdom from the experience so far. Here's what I've got:

Structure matters.

Going to an office every day has all kinds of advantages, but foremost among them is the structure it provides. You've got to get there, which requires the structure of a morning routine and the structure of a drive to work (you go the same way every time, right?). When you arrive there is a building and an office and a desk and a chair. There is coffee and a computer and a phone and books and paper. Oh, and there are people there who do things to support you if you ask nicely and treat them respectfully and return the favor once in a while. There are also people who work late at night to clean up after the other people, which is a pretty nice deal. Office structure is predictable and reliable. Mostly.

At my house...er, "home office," this is not always the case. There is definitely an existing structure but it is built and managed to run a family. Asking that same structure to also support a new business venture is a little like asking the dog to do the dishes. She's equipped in some ways... not so much in others. That said, I am an interloper in the household routines, useful on occasion – I spent much of my first week handling school drop-offs and pick-ups – and more of a redundant skulker in others, drinking coffee while the house moves into action around me.

At the office, you may or may not do your best work on any given day but the framework is there; the structure exists to support the possibility of something cool happening. At home, you control your destiny. You get to decide what happens when, what goes where, and whether or not you want to:

A) walk the dog

B) meditate

C) read

D) check for new blog subscribers (someone's reading this, right?)

F) play golf

G) write something (anything)

H) do the dishes (greatest form of procrastination ever because you feel so useful!)

I)   watch the clock for the socially acceptable hour to mix a cocktail

J)   make dinner (I barely could add this as it is such foreign territory)

K) call people who will generously validate your existence (thank you)

L) bemoan the ridiculously brief length of the modern school day…

You get the idea…

I'm a beginner at this, that much is clear. I need to allow myself some space to exist in the unknown, to bounce around a little while I sort it out. So far, what I can tell you is that an unstructured life is definitely worth living. It's just that you need some structure to pull it off.

One last observation about home office life: upon closer examination I have noticed that there is coffee and a computer and a phone and books and paper. Oh, and there are people there who do things to support you if you ask nicely and treat them respectfully and return the favor once in a while. There are also people who work late at night to clean up after the other people, which is a pretty nice deal.

Home office structure is predictable and reliable. Mostly.

"RULES FOR ART" REPURPOSED

{March 21, 2013}

...everyone is trying to create something and, in doing so, to connect to something larger than themselves. Some are more sophisticated and polished, others are rough and unrefined.

I attended my daughter's third grade Open House tonight. I learned about the "Rules for Art." With a little revision, it seems to be a pretty good list for leaders as well:

1. See that no one is perfect. Including yourself. Focus on each person's strengths and how they can creatively put them to work in service of the clear and compelling cause your organization stands for.

2. Be positive. There are plenty of reasons to get down and to assume the worst. Don't do it. Being positive doesn't mean you are unrealistic. It means you take your leadership responsibility seriously to set the tone for how the group as a whole – WE – are going to deal with this challenge.

3. Mistakes are a good thing. On the journey from the known (safety) to the unknown (risk, uncertainty, growth and change), you are going to make plenty of mistakes. If you don't, you are not actually on the journey. And if you're not on the journey, you're going to get passed by.

4. We will use materials properly. By doing so we recognize that we are not on an island, that our efforts to create are part of a larger system of creation that is counting on us to be mindful of the whole.

5. Respect everyone. Because everyone is trying to create something and, in doing so, to connect to something larger than themselves. Some are

sophisticated and polished, others are rough and unrefined. What if we assumed best intent and provided more space for them to grow into something even larger than they can currently imagine?

As I turned to leave the classroom I saw this on the opposite wall, a sign identifying the valued learning characteristic of the week:

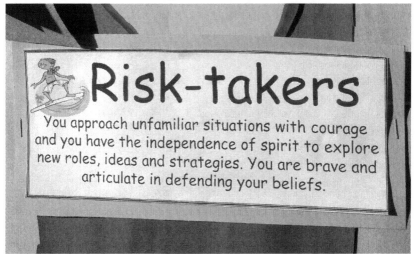

To lead by these "rules" is to stand for something that is both obvious and obviously unrealized. Doing so requires the brave articulation of something worth fighting for and the independence of spirit necessary to feel alone in pursuit of it.

To do so requires the very best kind of leadership.

MAKING IT UP AS YOU GO

{March 28, 2014}

You begin to feel a powerful discomfort with the seduction of the known and you find yourself straddling two worlds: one beckoning you back, the other calling you forward.

The problem with life is that there is no playbook. You arrive on the field and, if you're lucky, some nice people take care of you for a while and then, when you're old enough, you venture off to another part of the field and see what you can make of yourself. Still no playbook, but thoughts of possibilities abound. After a while longer, you figure out that in many ways it's easy, that most people "get it," and because they do, they drive on the right side of the road, pay their bills, and even hold the door open for you once in a while.

And then you decide to pursue one of those possibilities you dreamt up and you learn that it's not as easy as you thought, because now you're operating outside of the accepted behaviors of the many. You're hanging out on a part of the field that few, if any, have visited before. This is where it gets interesting because now you have a decision to make: will you stay long enough to sort it out, to make it up as you go and normalize this place? Will you keep discovering new parts of the field or will you retreat toward what you know because, after all, it's what you know? Typically, like most of those who have come this way before, you decide to go back, and you feel pretty good about this because it's predictable and understandable and allows you to fit in with the rest of the gang who are operating from the same set of rules.

Until they're not.

Because, of course, what you weren't banking on was that the rules you accepted as a "given" can change with more impact and velocity than you can possibly imagine. And they will. And they do. And now you're wondering which was the better deal: blindly expecting the known to remain the known so you could feel the false sense of safety you had learned to crave, or risking the responsibility of defining a new set of rules in an unknown territory, scaring yourself with the possibility of utter loss but wondering if that's not the point of the whole experience anyway.

The joy of life is that there is no playbook. You arrive on the field and, if you're lucky, some nice people take care of you for a while and then, when you're old enough, you venture off to another part of the field and see what you can make of yourself. You learn that you can create and so you keep venturing out, determining new rules as you go, experiencing new adventures, engaging new people, discovering new abilities and passions. You begin to feel a powerful discomfort with the seduction of the known and you find yourself straddling two worlds: one beckoning you back, the other calling you forward.

You get to decide…and it's the most important decision of your life.

RULES FOR MAKING IT UP AS YOU GO

{April 1, 2013}

At precisely the time that it feels like it's all about you, remind yourself that it absolutely is not.

Should you decide to go forward and say "yes" to the invitation from the unknown, here are a few "rules" I've been encouraged and challenged to follow by those who have stood in my corner:

1. First, know thyself. To put it bluntly, there's not much chance of you weathering the storm of isolation that comes with creating something new if you don't have a firm hold on who you are. By that I mean the vulnerability and awareness that comes from stretching yourself to really discover what makes you tick, at your best, your worst, and everywhere in between. Knowing this means you know what sets you off; how you react under pressure; how good you are when you're really good; how you respond to and recover from disappointment; how much tolerance you have for ambiguity, uncertainty, and the reality that the world is not going to roll over for you just because you'd like it to.

2. Stand on the shoulders of giants. Assemble the best group of supporters, mentors, teachers, coaches and friends you possibly can and use them as much as you can. What's the point of having people in your life who truly care about your success if you're not willing to ask them for help? Take stock of those you most rely on. If this group doesn't inspire, challenge and implore you; doesn't push, cajole, beckon and admonish you in the best, least comfortable way (meaning, they actually tell you the truth) to be the person you are most afraid of being; well then, you'd better find a new crowd.

3. Practice courage every day. You don't have to win every day. You just have to practice. Small acts of well-placed, well-timed insubordination against the known and the expected are exceptional ways of reminding yourself that (A) you are, indeed, alive, and (B) you can break away from the pack and plant a new crop of awesomeness in YOUR section of the field. I'm talking about mild and enjoyable insurrections like striking up a conversation with someone you don't know or practicing a new discipline even though you are confident you will be terrible at it (meditation comes to mind). It might be starting a blog or volunteering to help kids or anything that requires you to get out of your own way, get a little exposed, and wrestle with the unknown.

4. It's not all about you. At precisely the time that it feels like it is all about you (you're exploring the undiscovered country, right? you're moving towards this big, scary risk, aren't you? your well-being is on the line, isn't it?), remind yourself that it absolutely is not. It's all about everybody else and what you can do for them. In my family, we like to say "give a little, get a little." It means that the world is reciprocal and you've got to go first. No matter what.

5. Go slow to go fast. My guess is that if you know you've got something important to create, some new possibility to bring to life that's got you tied up in knots, you have spent considerable time thinking about how big and scary it all is without doing much about it. You know, of course (because everybody does) that small steps are essential to getting the snowball started. By this I mean those seemingly insignificant acts (and funny, isn't it, how we tell ourselves that they are insignificant because they are "small" and "small" is just so undervalued in our culture even though anyone – ANYONE – who ever accomplished anything worth writing about will tell you that they started small?) that are related, directly or indirectly, to your larger purpose.

TELEPHONE POLES, FENCE POSTS AND RAILROAD TIES

{June 1, 2013}

You know exactly what to do. There's no need to be afraid. Keep walking.

I routinely make the mistake of downloading hundreds of podcasts to my iPhone because I have no clue how to successfully navigate the new iTunes interface. The old one was fine and I am slow to change. So be it.

Scrolling through hundreds of recordings the other day – none of which I've ever listened to – I came across This American Life episode #494: "Hit the Road." The first story is of a young man, Andrew Forsthoefel, who, upon losing his job, decides to walk from Philadelphia to the Pacific Ocean wearing a sign that says, "Walking to Listen." It's an incredible, beautifully told adventure and one you deserve to hear for plenty of reasons, especially for his interview with a 73-year-old man named Otho Rogers of Melrose, New Mexico.

Mr. Rogers reflects ruefully and with a searing honesty on the passage of time and his personal loss of physical ability. You ache with him when he describes the shame of having to climb a fence rail to mount his horse when all he wants is to be able to get his foot in the stirrup and haul himself up the way he used to do in his strong and effortless youth.

Mr. Rogers goes on to describe our shifting perspectives on time as we age as the difference between viewing telephone poles, fence posts and railroad ties as you drive along the road. The longer we live, the less space there is between each marker: telephone poles in our youth; fence posts in midlife; railroad ties in our old age. The accelerating vehicle that is our life gets moving so quickly with the accumulation of time that the railroad ties themselves become just a blur.

We come to know in a real and often painful way that time is both unstoppable and completely unsympathetic to our plight: that we have what we have and how we spend it is completely up to us.

Inspired by Otho Rogers and others he meets along the way, Mr. Forsthoefel finally shares his own response to a question he asked of many others along his route: *"What advice would you give to your younger self?"*

His answer is a guide for all of us, whether we are counting by poles, posts or ties.

"You know exactly what to do. There's no need to be afraid. Keep walking."

THE LONG WAY HOME

{June 30, 2013}

As I was catching my breath and feeling alive with the energy of my exertion, I couldn't help but consider the road not taken.

In San Francisco last week I had dinner one evening on the Embarcadero, near the refurbished Southern Pacific building at the foot of Market Street. Following the meal, I was eager to stretch my legs and enjoy the waterfront, prepared to hail a cab when I'd had enough walking. The sky was bright on this early summer evening and I was enjoying my stroll back to the home of my friend who was generously putting me up. She lives off of Broadway, on the other side of one of the city's most notorious hills. By the time I got through the red light district, the south edge of North Beach, and into Chinatown, I realized that this was becoming much more than an after-dinner stroll. By the time I reached the set of stairs built into the sidewalk to compensate for the severity of the slope, I was in a full sweat.

Just prior to taking on this last ascent – one climb to go – I decided to take a look back at where I had been. As I briefly contemplated my new perspective on one of the most beautiful cities in the world, as I was catching my breath and feeling alive with the energy of my exertion, I couldn't help but consider the road not taken.

Shortcuts are tempting and often satisfying. They emphasize speed and completion, holding the promise of getting on to the next thing without undue delay. They also have a way of devaluing the experience of the journey. They can rob us of the power of the present moment and the opportunity, in the fullness of time, to experience something unexpected and deeply gratifying.

Sometimes you've got to go over instead of through.

LEARNING STARTS WITH YES

{September 9, 2013}

...her courage to be a beginner is a great reminder that within each of us is the possibility of becoming something greater, if only we are willing to say yes.

Two recent personal examples illustrate this point:

1. My son is not the most skilled player on his soccer team. He is a great all-around athlete and has years of recreation league soccer experience, but with only a seasonal interest in the game, he has not developed the finer skills of ball control. He is now playing on a club team, which is why the skill gap has become more obvious. Most of his teammates have been playing competitive soccer for a few years and they have honed abilities that are pretty impressive. Since it's my son's first year on the team – and since he joined a winning team – he's not getting much playing time; probably 15 minutes out of a 70-minute game. The progression of his attitude about this has been a wonderful thing to observe. At first, he was intimidated by his teammate's abilities and when the ball came his way he would get rid of it as quickly as possible for fear of messing up. Now that the season is well underway, it is so much fun to watch the transformation of both his attitude and his confidence. It's not that his skills have caught-up to those of the other boys; it's how badly he wants to get into the game and how willingly he wants to contribute. About midway through the first half of a recent game, I heard his coach call his name, immediately followed by an emphatic, fist pumping "Yes!" from my son.

I'm excited for his growth as a player and a person; I'm especially grateful to have such a great model of hard work and passion from someone who, like all of us, still has so much to learn.

2. We recently purchased a "lovingly used" piano we found on Craigslist. It's in great shape and is the perfect instrument for our daughter who, after a few years of lessons and a clearly developing musical interest and ability, is ready to graduate from an electronic keyboard to a "real" piano. What we didn't count on is that her older sister would also express an interest in our new piece of musical furniture. She kept hanging around it and making up songs until one day I asked her, just for fun and with zero expectation, if she would like to learn how to play. To my great surprise, she said, "Yes." What makes this a surprising response is that my daughter is very sensitive and cautious about trying new things. She does not want to look bad and she is deeply aware that being a beginner is a sure way to look silly. Within this context, her saying yes to trying out piano lessons is a pretty remarkable turn of events. It may be that she's just being competitive with her little sister. Or it may be that she's turned a corner in the battle to more firmly establish her self-esteem, to more confidently take on life's slings and arrows. Whatever the reason, her courage to be a beginner is inspiring and, while unexpected, a great reminder that within each of us is the possibility of becoming something greater, if only we are willing to say yes.

Learning is the only path through change. To what new learning opportunity will you respond, "Yes!" in the week ahead?

LEARNING STARTS WITH YES (UPDATED)

{September 10, 2013}

Children haven't been around long enough to understand that, as George Lucas once said, "We're all living in cages with the door wide open."

When my youngest child learned that her older siblings had been featured in dad's recent blog post, she was not upset at being left out, just curious as to why she was not included. You see, she reminded me, just two weeks ago she started at a brand new school because over the summer her mom, an experienced educator (and really good mom), described to her that this new school would be a much better environment for her specific learning needs. To this my daughter had simply replied, "Yes."

She didn't allow the fear of change, the discomfort of new surroundings, or the absence of old friends to deter her from agreeing to try something new. And, I'm proud to say, it's a pretty solid eight-year-old who can look at those realities and say yes anyway.

Two takeaways: First, there is "yes" happening all around us. Take a look around and get yourself inspired. Second, as all three of my examples demonstrate, "yes" is disproportionately more likely to come from the mouths of children than of adults. Sure, it's easier for them. They're not up against mortgages and medical bills and the emotional and financial challenges of caring for kids and parents, alike. In short, they haven't been around long enough to understand that, as George Lucas once said, "We're all living in cages with the door wide open" For them, there is no cage. We have a lot to learn from their yes, maybe most importantly to stop making excuses and get on with our learning.

Oh, and one more thing: my daughter asked if she could also write a blog. A blog about princesses.

I said, "Yes. Yes you can."

PRESENT CREATION, FUTURE CREATIVITY

{November 13, 2013}

What is newly created today will not remain intact...it can be multiplied in its usefulness as it is claimed for new purposes and possibilities.

This is "Heartlake High School," the new Lego set my daughter earned by giving up thumb sucking. Her future orthodontist encouraged us to reward her if she could go an entire month without sucking her thumb and she did! And so we did. She spent nearly an entire day building it, playing with it, deconstructing it and reconstructing it. (Me: "Have you taken a break today?" Her: "Mom made me stop and have lunch.") She loves this Lego set.

This is the Tech center, a "state of the art" technology classroom created by my other daughter, inspired as she was by her sister's new construction. The keen observer will notice a few laptops, study materials and a special couch just for the teacher. Equally obsessed with her task, she, too, spent the day in building mode making multiple trips to the big Lego box upstairs for additional resources.

For a good six hours the girls played, created, enjoyed and engaged. No dustups, no frustration, no rivalry. Just play. It was the best kind of engagement.

Both of their creations are brilliant. And they are quite different, aren't they? I have always cherished the brand new Lego set and the chance to build with exactitude what's pictured on the box. My daughter did so brilliantly, one page and one piece at a time. I have also loved turning a random assortment of parts into something different and new, something you can only realize through imagination, trial and error, and the patience required to sift through old parts in search of just the right piece.

And this is why Lego is so dang smart. They know that we want both. They know that we want to make what's on the box AND that, slowly but surely, those parts are going to make their way into the big box of "previously new" creations and become components for future, unscripted endeavors. What both Lego creators and our children  understand implicitly is that, as gratifying as it is to fully realize the new set, it's only going to be the new set for a little while. What is newly created today will not remain intact. The new becomes the used with the predictability of waves hitting the shoreline. As it does, it can be multiplied in its usefulness as it is claimed for new purposes and possibilities.

As leaders, we are charged with facilitating our team's creation of the new just as we are charged with helping them learn from its deconstruction and dissemination into future endeavors, commensurate with the critical necessity to continuously repurpose our best work in response to the next evolution of demand. Yes, some things are built to last – things like relationship, connection, trust and creativity.

Everything else should be tossed into the big box, refreshing the supply of old elements waiting to be reborn into new creations.

IF MORE LEADERS
HAD THE COURAGE
MY 8-YEAR-OLD
DAUGHTER RECENTLY
DISPLAYED, THE
WORLD WOULD BE A
BETTER PLACE. AND
NOT JUST BY A
LITTLE BIT.

COURAGE

{December 10, 2013}

A few months ago, as I was researching recreational basketball sign-ups for my 13-year-old son, I randomly, impulsively and somewhat jokingly asked my daughters if they would also like to sign up. One said yes and one said no. I had no expectation of a yes from either of them as their single, previous foray into team sports was not a rousing success. Not in the winning/losing sense of it, but more in the, "I don't like soccer because there's too much running" sense. We chalked it up as a new experience, reminded ourselves it's not for everybody and got on with life.

But, this time, something made me issue the invitation and no one was more surprised than me to get that yes from my 8-year-old. In the weeks between signing up and waiting for a coach to call, we occasionally played basketball together in the driveway and it was clear that this was something she was genuinely interested in doing. I was thrilled, and not because I see her in the WNBA someday, but because this daughter of mine is an expert solo practitioner – an awesome reader, wonderful piano player, and possessed of a rich and vivid imagination – who I think will benefit enormously from the social, collaborative and competitive necessities of a team sport.

What I failed to anticipate is that she equated basketball with hanging out one-on-one with dad in the driveway and not with some noisy, musty gymnasium full of other kids who were all "better than her." In her enthusiasm, I failed to remember her fear.

And so it was that when we arrived at her first practice and the girls were goofing around and shooting baskets before getting started, she was more than content to sit with me on the sidelines. When her coach finally brought the kids together, he asked the girls to sit together on the court while he spoke to the parents. While he covered his basic philosophy of teaching basketball to kids ("I just want them to learn to love the game") I noticed that her anxiety was visibly increasing.

Finally, parents dispersing to the sidelines and girls lining up on the baseline, my daughter's moment of truth had come. She was going to play basketball. She was crestfallen; so sad and so alone. She was doing her best impression of bravery, quivering lip and all, discreetly wiping away her tears.

But she didn't run to me. She stood in her spot, felt her feelings, and, as things got underway, joined in quickly and actively. She excelled at the various drills, took instruction well and soon learned that she was neither the worst nor the best one there. She had a great time.

She felt the fear and acted anyway. She displayed the courage to learn, the courage to try, the courage to fail, the courage to just show up and be counted, and, finally, the courage to recognize that her feelings – aloneness, sadness, vulnerability – were a real and necessary part of the experience, companions that remind us that we are exactly where we are supposed to be.

WHEN IN DOUBT, SHUT UP AND LISTEN

{February 6, 2014}

When you find yourself in an unexpected situation, it never hurts to remind yourself that it's not all about you.

On Tuesday evening this week, I found myself onstage with legendary sports broadcaster Dick Enberg and Hall of Fame basketball player Bill Walton. My role was to moderate a conversation about what it takes to be a "game changer" with two people who have seen, experienced and created countless game-changing moments at both the collegiate and professional level. This conversation was held in the context of a servant leadership conference, the goal of which was to educate and challenge participants to go out and "change the game" in their organizations by leading both from the heart and the head.

Photo credit: Dennis Baggett

I was never supposed to be there. I was pinch-hitting, informed a day earlier that I was filling in for the conference host who had fallen ill. I was stepping in for a man who was missing out on the chance to talk with two of his childhood heroes; I can only imagine his disappointment.

Instead, they got me.

Was I nervous? At first, I thought I would and should be. After all, I was going to talk with two legends, on camera, under the lights, and in front of about 300 people. But the more I considered it, the more I realized I wasn't nervous at all. Not one bit.

Here's why:

I know Dick Enberg and Bill Walton. Not personally, of course, but for the purpose of a 75-minute conversation, I reminded myself of what I did know: first, Dick Enberg is a broadcaster, for goodness sake! He's been talking for a living for nearly 50 years. And Bill Walton is one of, if not the most, verbose people you could ever possibly encounter. They had a half-century of experiences to share and they didn't need any help from me.

When you find yourself in an unexpected situation, even a little bit of information counts for a lot.

I knew the subject matter. I was a co-host for the conference, and even though this particular session wasn't on my duty roster, I had certainly given some thought to the relationship between effective leadership and athletic achievement. For what it's worth, the conference was held next door to a baseball stadium with the theme, "Changing the Game." I figured that, with even limited preparation and a little imagination, I could find my way into and through a meaningful conversation.

When you find yourself in an unexpected situation, trust your competence.

I know when to shut-up and listen. The fact is, I was completely superfluous to the discussion. Besides some brief and respectful introductory remarks and something similar at the end, I asked two questions in 75 minutes. Did I know that Dick and Bill had known each other for over 40 years? Nope. Did I know that they were proud members of the mutual admiration society? Nope. Did I know that they would set one another up for anecdote after anecdote, layering one story on top of another as if constructing a perfect lasagna? Nope. So I shut-up and listened, enjoying the fact that I had the best seat in the house and deciding to make the most of it. The accompanying photo here makes it look like I was smoothly in charge of the whole affair, coolly brandishing my microphone in between thoughtful questions and dialogue with a couple of superstars. It was no such thing. A picture taken at the right time can make anything seem true.

When you find yourself in an unexpected situation, sometimes you just need to shut up and listen.

At one point during the event, Bill Walton told a story about a guy who was moderating a conversation he was a part of when he stopped mid-sentence, pointed at me and said, "Kind of like Kevin is supposed to be doing!" As the crowd laughed I attempted to remind him that my name is "David" only to have Dick Enberg chime in with, "You're the most overpaid guy in the room!" A very funny moment. A great dose of humility.

When you find yourself in an unexpected situation, it never hurts to remind yourself that it's not all about you.

It really never is.

NOT EVERY DAY
BREAKS AS PLANNED.
SOMETIMES, IF
WE STICK WITH
IT, A LITTLE GOOD
FORTUNE COMES
OUR WAY.

SOMETIMES

{December 2, 2014}

Sometimes you meet some nice people and they invite you to teach a class in their organization.

Sometimes they ask you to do that on the first Tuesday in December.

Sometimes you decide to make it an out-and-back trip because the United Airlines schedule makes that possible.

Sometimes your morning flight leaves at 6:45 so you set your alarm clock for 4:15.

Sometimes you mistakenly set your alarm clock for 4:15 on Thursday when your flight is on Tuesday.

Sometimes you get to sleep extra early on Monday to make sure you are in one piece after getting up at 4:15 on Tuesday.

Sometimes, by the sheer grace of God and all of the positive forces in the universe combined and concentrated in your favor, your body decides to wake up at 4:56 on Tuesday because it knows you have to be somewhere even though you've made a grievous error in setting your alarm.

Sometimes, between 4:56 and 5:12 on the first Tuesday in December, you shower, shave, dress, and drive away from your home praying for (A) no traffic and (B) no rain.

Sometimes you are grateful that the traffic doesn't start that early and the rain doesn't either.

Sometimes you park your car at 5:52 for a flight that boards at 6:10, praying this time for a fast security line.

Sometimes, many times on this day, your prayers are answered and at 6:05 you are making small talk with the cashier at Peet's because you are steps away from your gate and you are in Boarding Group 5.

Sometimes you nearly finish your coffee while waiting to board your flight because United Airlines is still trying to figure out how to expedite the boarding process.

Sometimes you sit down in your assigned seat and give thanks for how fortunate you are to be alive, to be present, and to be on your way to do the work you believe in.

Sometimes you celebrate with shrimp étouffée and a tall beer in the Houston Airport.

Sometimes you are headed home.

CONDITIONS FOR CREATIVITY

{February 3, 2015}

We create the conditions for creativity when we sit in the chair and do the work.

I've been doing a lot of writing recently, which is to say that I've been more consistently inviting my creative self to come out and play. I have noticed that my creativity is a willing companion so long as a few key conditions are met.

First, consistency matters. Every day, even for a short time, I invite my creativity to spend some time with me. It's usually at about the same time of day, in the same quiet room. There's usually coffee and a comfortable chair. She likes that very much.

Second, she is more playful, I've noticed, when I'm less judgmental, more loving. In fact, she has a particular affinity for resting on my chest so she can find the rhythm of my heartbeat rather than on my head where she can only hear the clanging calculations of doubt.

She is shy, my creative self, especially in the presence of negativity. Comparison sends her running. She doesn't "do" Facebook.

I've noticed that she keeps her head in the clouds, searching for meaning and marvel, and her feet in the dirt, softly vigilant in the name of doing the work.

And, with deep empathy she forgives, again and again, my flight into dish-doing, tax-organizing, invoice-sending, laundry-folding and the innumerable ways I find to satisfy my outcome-oriented, completion-focused, messiness-averting self.

She is a faithful friend, my creativity. I strive to be her worthy companion.

WALKING

{February 4, 2015}

I have walked myself into my best thoughts.

– Søren Kierkegaard

I have lost count of the number of times I have sat slumped at my desk at an impasse with a project, proposal, or blog post only to finally admit that my best and only option is to extract myself from the chair, put on my walking shoes, get a leash on the dog and head out for a walk.

Slogging through it. Grinding it out. Trying harder. These all have their place. But without a sustained attention to the energy they demand, their gravitational pull can lead us into a one-dimensional orbit of limited perspective.

When I get up and get moving, I invite my body to join my brain in a conversation of possibility. Turning hard questions over in my mind, my movement acts as a sharp spade, knifing through the impacted soil of my narrowed thought. I open up the gravelly earth of my thinking and dis-cover what is hidden there, what can only be found with the gifts of space, movement, air and sun.

Inevitably, I surprise myself with a key word or thought that feels so obvious and clear that I can only wonder why I waited so long to get this change of scenery.

Sometimes, instead of insisting on figuring it out in a sustained glut of effort, the best I can do is to create the conditions most likely to aid my search for a new way forward.

We were not made for slumping in chairs. We were made to move.

STAYING CLOSE
TO THE HARDEST
THING IS A SURE
WAY TO STAY IN A
CONVERSATION OF
POSSIBILITY.

THE BOULDER NEXT DOOR

{February 9, 2015}

Obstacles aren't always to be simply overcome. They also need to be understood. Keeping a close relationship with what is in our way does not mean that we are giving in to its power. It can mean that we have made friends with it in such a way that we are challenged to discover a creative response to a difficult reality.

There are boulders. They are large, heavy, even ominous. They do not always have to be moved.

When we reach out to what most impedes our growth, there is the very real possibility that we will form a new relationship with it. We might even learn to shake hands with it each day in recognition of its potential to overwhelm us. We respect its necessary placement as the thing we need to come up against in order to sharpen our resolve, to clarify our response to the continuous truth of unwelcome but necessary challenges.

We may find that in our striving to go through, the best answer is often to find a way around. This is slower, plodding, and frustrating to our need to figure out, complete, achieve and finish. But it also may create opportunity for a new perspective that serves to deepen the empathy we hold for ourselves.

When we find that we are clinging to something unmovable, it can be easy to forget that we are still growing.

Staying close to the hardest thing is a sure way to stay in a conversation of possibility. Over time, we may find that what was once immovable has moved us in ways we could not have done without.

VENTURE CAPITAL

{February 20, 2015}

They will be energized by your choice and magnetized by
your purpose.

The venture is where you decide to go.

The capital is what you're willing to spend to get there.

My sense of it is that when you decide to fund yourself, others will fund you also. They won't be able to help themselves. They will be energized by your choice and magnetized by your purpose. You will be irresistible and they won't want to look away.

But never forget: you're not doing it for them.

Venture well. Spend heavily. You can't take it with you.

TAKE COVER

{February 22, 2015}

Seek shelter when needed and then get right back out in the sun. Too much is waiting for you. Even the scary stuff.

Moss is a simple plant that needs plenty of water and lots of shade. In the Northern Hemisphere, it mostly grows on the north side of trees, rocks, and buildings because it is hiding from the sun.

Sometimes you are a simple moss, hiding from the torchlight of your reality in hopes that it will pass you by.

Sometimes you are a complex, vascular being who grows boldly into the light in pursuit of bigger things.

Sometimes you take cover to hide from the things that scare you.

Sometimes you take cover to replenish and restore so that you can meet those very things with a new resolve.

The good work is to stay clear about the difference.

FROM THE KNOWN AT THE CENTER OF YOUR EXPERIENCE TO THE EDGE OF POSSIBILITY.

SACRED DISTANCE

{February 17, 2015}

From the head to the heart.

From where you are to where you want to go.

From the known at the center of your experience to the edge of possibility.

From the tyranny of scarcity to the liberation of plenty.

Any authentic effort to cover this ground is a holy act.
There is no greater work.

PROPHETS, BY THEIR VERY NATURE, CAN'T BE RIGHT AT THE CENTER OF THE SOCIAL STRUCTURE...

ON THE EDGE OF THE INSIDE

{February 18, 2015}

...They cannot be full insiders, but they cannot throw rocks from outside either. Their structural position to this day is 'on the edge of the inside.' You must know and live the essential rules before you can critique what is not essential or not as important.

– Richard Rohr

I invite you to consider the ways – through the lens of a very particular example – you play the role of priest or prophet in your own practice of leadership. Do you find yourself leading in service of maintaining systemic order or in service of disrupting the status quo in support of a larger ideal?

Let's remember our history right from the start: most prophets get killed. In spite of the intention that prophets would serve as a balance to the formal structures of the early church, their role as disrupters would often become too much – too uncomfortable – for the kings and priests whose job was to hold the whole thing together.

The demanding realities of organizational systems – especially the dynamic realities of hierarchy, power, and control – make it laughable to some to even consider this conversation. Understandably, most leaders don't want to get killed. It seems to me, though, that the focus on avoiding death is alarmingly disproportionate to the energy required to define what it is the leader is going to live and lead for.

In that focus on the avoidance of death – and in the absence of higher calling – comes the worst kind of loyalty, acquiescence to the seat of authority that granted the promotion in the first place. This misplaced loyalty comes at a steep organizational cost as the needs of the entire system, the stated ideals and vision of the enterprise, are so frequently sacrificed at the altar of personal gain.

Our organizations must not just tolerate but actively cultivate prophets, those precious few who can operate "on the edge of the inside," serving the system by maintaining a remove that allows for a healthy and constructive critique of just how far it may have strayed from its stated ideals. Essentially, this is about the courage and ability – and potentially the self-sacrifice – to hold the system in a conversation about the distance between where it is and where it says it wants to go.

It is not idealistic to say that a balance between priest and prophet is attainable. It is simply a decision to be made by those in the "seat of power" to no longer view their position as a one-dimensional construct that occasionally tolerates outside perspectives as an exercise of "inclusion" or "diversity." It is a decision to be lived out through thousands upon thousands of daily behaviors that promote tolerance, strive for understanding, enhance learning, open dialogue, challenge perspectives, and energize commitment. Yes, a big decision, but a decision just the same.

Once again, do you find yourself leading in service of maintaining systemic order or in service of disrupting the status quo in support of a larger ideal?

IF ONLY

{February 26, 2015}

...we can tell ourselves a new story of possibility...or we can tell ourselves an old story of the way the game is played and let "if only" rule the day.

The best way to prevent yourself from accomplishing anything worthwhile is to get stuck in the land of "if only."

If only I had more experience. If only I had more connections. If only she would talk to me. If only they didn't think that. If only I had more training. If only I had more time. If only I didn't have these other commitments. If only I was lucky. If only I were more skilled. If only I were a better writer, speaker, dancer, marketer, programmer, facilitator, presenter, resumé writer, researcher, singer, networker, leader, etc.

The biggest problem with a world in which the rules of the game are changing so dramatically is that we have to create a new story about how to navigate it. And it is only a story. The sooner we grasp that "it's all invented" and that we are experts at constructing our own meanings and our own realities, the sooner we get to decide what to do with that extraordinary insight.

One option is that we can tell ourselves a new story of possibility. Another is that we can tell ourselves an old story of the way the game is played and let "if only" rule the day.

One of three things is true:

1)   You've got what you need at least to get started and you are afraid that it's insufficient for what the world expects.

2)   You know what you need to get started – new information, skills, relationships – and now you've got to go get it.

3)   You don't know what you need because you don't know what you want.

You either need to get moving, get learning or get clear. If only there were another way.

ROOM TO RUN

{March 16, 2015}

Always this energy smolders inside, when it remains unlit
the body fills with dense smoke.

– David Whyte

You have more freedom than you think you do. This is the strange
dilemma we face in a society of wide-open access to information, of infinite
do-it-yourself possibilities. We have all the freedom we need except for
where we need it most: behind our eyes and between our ears.

I heard a piece on the radio yesterday about the power of exposure to
open up the imagination to what is possible. If I see bigger, I might live bigger. If I see freedom, I might pursue freedom. If I see wealth, opportunity,
advancement – a concrete example of another way forward – I might reason
that it can exist for me also and then take action to achieve it.

Any opening to another way, however slender it might be, is enough to
get some people to leap. Others, not so much. Most of us remain bound by
our perceptions, locked into mindsets that make sense to us, well-shaped
by years of effort. While we maintain an inner dialogue of, "This is what
I know, so this is what I am," smoldering inside is a tiny fire of possibility that is screaming for oxygen. Remaining unlit, it streams toxic smoke
throughout our bodies, directly to our heads, flooding our hearts.

It may be that you don't think you're worthy of your freedom.

You may believe that how you use your freedom won't pass the test of
others' care and concern.

Or, very likely, the room you want – the freedom you crave – belongs to a group of "insiders," smart and special people who have what it takes and have "earned" their keys to a door you're still fumbling to find.

There's never been a time like this. What are you going to do about that?

Rita doesn't get off the leash too often. When she does, she makes the most of it.

YOUR CROOKED PATH

{March 26, 2015}

If you're still playing, you've already won. Now that that's out of the way, what are you going to do about it?

Seems like a good time to stop telling ourselves that old story of how it's all supposed to turn out.

You get to define "winning."

You get to choose how to walk the path to get there.

You get to decide how to deal with your feelings of insecurity, inadequacy, loneliness and frustration.

You also get to decide how to share your feelings of gratitude, energy, joy and fulfillment.

Feeling those feelings, tossing around in the messy middle between the poles of jubilation and desperation, is precisely how you know you are on your own crooked path.

If you're still playing, you've already won. Now that that's out of the way, what are you going to do about it?

INTERSECTIONS

{April 8, 2015}

You won't know until you start walking.

The more you keep moving, the more intersections you will come to. The more intersections you come to, the more choices you will have. The more choices you have, the more possibility you will discover.

You can choose to wade into shallow water that will quickly become deep. Perhaps you are called to do something that frightens you, that threatens to overwhelm you. And it might. Or it might buoy you, turning into a swift current that carries you to what you long for. You won't know until you plunge in.

You can choose to walk on the soft sand, each footstep sinking in and pulling you down. Perhaps you are called to reconnect to something you once cherished, a place or relationship to which you hope to belong in a new way. The sand may exhaust you. Or it may turn to firmer earth that supports a quicker pace. You won't know until you start walking.

You can choose to scale the rough wall, each hand and foothold scraping at your resolve. Perhaps you are called to confront an old belief, a tired adaptation that begs to be released. The wall may daunt you, its vertical certainty demanding every ounce of your limited commitment. Or it may at last offer an unobstructed view that leads to a new understanding. You won't know until you start climbing.

Keep moving forward, turning toward the choices that unlock the possibility of your life.

I HEARD THE
QUESTION
UNDERNEATH THE
QUESTION: WHAT
GIVES YOU THE RIGHT
TO THINK YOU CAN
DO THIS?

WHO DO YOU THINK YOU ARE?

{April 9, 2015}

For what feels like a very long time, especially in my late twenties and well into my thirties, I was asked this question a lot. And every time I was asked, I heard it as an accusation, for I thought I heard the real question underneath the question, "What gives you the right to think you can do this?"

Wide-eyed, naïve, and guilty, I would inevitably respond with some stammered version of "I don't know" or "I'm figuring that out" or "I think it's this" or "It might be that." My answer was always a plea for mercy from the smallest part of myself.

Strangely, I was only asked the question at times when I was attempting something new, stretching out, exploring new space; maybe with writing or speaking, perhaps with a new workshop design. Unfailingly, the question would be asked of me during conversations with "smart" people about books or movies or politics. It would always be asked in charged meetings where points of view were expected or positions were being staked out.

Always, the question would come.

One day I started to look out for the people who would ask it. I started to wise up and get ready for it because I could predict who it would come from and when. The more I paid attention, the more I noticed that the people who would ask this question shared similar qualities: tone of voice, style of dress, demeanor, and even size and shape.

Again and again and again, the people who would ask this question all looked eerily familiar to me.

And then, one day, I saw it clearly. The people asking this question – those judgmental, insensitive, thoughtless, discouraging people – were actually only one person in many different guises.

The reason they looked so familiar was that they were all me.

DEVELOPING YOUR VOICE OF EXPLORATION

As we are willing to explore ourselves and to connect with others, we become more willing to explore our world. Being willing to explore the world – by which I mean our present circumstances and our pressing questions – from a posture of curiosity and learning is essential to leading necessary change.

Just as we may ask of ourselves, "Who am I being?" and "How did I come to be this way?" and "How might I be an even better version of myself?," we need to ask the same of our teams and our institutions. The Voice of Exploration implies a commitment to questioning the status quo, not just for the sake of doing so, but out of a keen awareness that our very human tendency is to settle into patterns that easily become ruts. Those ruts are the greatest inhibitors of change, particularly in light of the fact that we so often don't even know we are in them!

Some practices to consider for bringing the Voice of Exploration alive in yourself and within those you lead:

– At the beginning of every project, hold a "premortem" meeting in which all concerns and possible challenges can be expressed and anticipated.

– At the end of every project, hold a "postmortem" meeting to uncover the insights that need to be memorized for future work.

Model questioning. Ask every team member in every one-on-one or group interaction what he or she sees that has become stale or dusty and what he or she would do about it

- No sacred cows. Take a critical eye, and do this often, to what's working well. Put it under the microscope and see if you can notice any threats lurking in the shadows. What are the stories you are telling yourself about this particular thing? What power have you given it over your perspective and your judgment about what is best for the organization?

- Learn something new. Whether it's work related or not, be a continuous learner to maintain your own "beginner's mindset" and to cultivate that ongoing sensibility within the group. Celebrate new learning, experimentation, and discovery on a regular basis.

- Take a walk in the woods. Or around the city. Or around a new neighborhood. Leave the maps and smartphones at home. Go and have a direct experience of being an explorer. See what happens.

- Visit a playground. Observe the kids at play. What do they have to teach you?

AFTERWORD

My voice is born repeatedly in the fields of uncertainty,
                                    – *Terry Tempest Williams*

A More Daring Life

We have to rethink what it means to be safe. As much as we might like it to, safety no longer means predictable and comfortable, linear and clean. It no longer means protected and certain, constant and available. It does not and it cannot. The stakes are just too high.

For those who are willing to embrace it, the new definition of safety starts with freedom. It is the freedom earned when we can confidently and clearly speak with our voices of understanding, connection and exploration.

We are safe when we can articulate our Voice of Understanding, knowing ourselves and using that awareness to stand more confidently in the face of complexity and change.

By doing so, we grant ourselves safety from a life of limited perspective and unrealized potential.

We are safe when we can articulate our Voice of Connection, opening ourselves to others, connecting and relating so that we can help one another navigate the realities of complexity and change.

By doing so, we grant ourselves safety from the loneliness and exhaustion of going it alone.

We are safe when we can articulate our Voice of Exploration, pursuing our edges so that we can discover new possibilities in the face of complexity and change.

By doing so, we grant ourselves safety from the seduction of the status quo, the real peril of thinking we have it all figured out.

The only true safety is that which comes from leading a more daring life.

It is not granted. It is earned.

And it is available to all of us.

HOW ARE YOU LEADING A MORE DARING LIFE?

An invitation to share your experience:

There is one piece of feedback, one specific comment I can always count on when I ask groups of leaders to discuss and share their experiences with one another. Following their conversations, I ask them to articulate what they have gained from talking with their colleagues, and at least one person will say that the benefit of the conversation is "finding out that I'm not alone." Nodding in agreement, others will add that the importance of spending time learning from one another is the comfort and aid of discovering how much they have in common, how many of their challenges are the same.

The demands of leadership are difficult for all of us. There is a powerful solace in knowing that we are not alone in striving to meet them well.

In the spirit of that repeated experience and in an effort to further explore the truth that what is personal and particular is, indeed, universal, I extend you the following invitation:

Please send me any anecdotes or stories that illustrate your own experience of developing and speaking your voices of understanding, connection and exploration.

You might share a practice you employ, a time when you learned a tough lesson, or an achievement or insight that evolved from your efforts. My goal is to create a repository of these stories to be featured in future blog posts and other publications with full credit to their source or in complete anonymity, whichever is your preference.

If you are willing to share your experiences, please send me an email at david@rule13learning.com.

Your contributions will help all of us to continue moving toward deeper understanding and greater impact.

I look forward to our correspondence.

ACKNOWLEDGEMENTS

What I need is someone who will make me do what I can.

– Ralph Waldo Emerson

One day, Steve Murphy suggested that I turn my blog into a book. It was just what I needed to make a start. As I shared the idea – selectively, tentatively – with other close friends, it was met with a quality of encouragement that both inspired and sustained me. Thank you, Steve and thanks, also, to Felicia Lee, Molly Davis, Alia Fitzgerald, Jeff Shuck and Jennifer Hadley for your untempered and persistent "Go for it!"

As I worked to find my direction a number of people provided the compass I so often could not find. In their reading of early drafts JaRae Birkeland, Molly Davis, Alia Fitzgerald, Steve Loy, Rita Patel, and Ken Van Kampen thoughtfully and firmly got me back to the main road. And when I resisted getting back to work, I envisioned Kelly Younger at his writing desk and Stephanie Younger knocking on yet another door. Thank you for reminding me what commitment looks like. I am grateful, also, to Kathlyn Hyatt Stewart for her careful editing and thoughtful shaping of the manuscript.

Ten years ago, when I went to work at TaylorMade-adidas Golf Company, I met a group of people who unknowingly became the "Committee to Open David Berry's Eyes to What is Possible." When you don't know what you don't know it's especially helpful to meet a group of brilliant people who are both willing and able to pull back the curtain. Blake McHenry, Cal Harrah, Marlene Laping, Sheila Sharpe, and Gary Heil helped me into bigger conversations than I knew were necessary or possible. Empathy and intellect were married in their generous commitment to my learning.

And to all of my colleagues at TaylorMade, and all of the leaders with whom I have worked before and since, thank you for encouraging and challenging me. Thank you for trusting me with your confidence. It was among and because of you that these ideas began to shape the work of my life and the life of my work.

To my children, whose lives and love comfort and challenge me every day:

- Duncan, your enthusiasm for new experiences is inspiring. I so admire your energy and your maturity...the really impressive ways you are taking responsibility for your life.

- Avery, you remind me every day that "conventional" and "amazing" have nothing in common. You see things other can't see. You handle things others can't handle. Keep going. You are a creative problem solver and the world needs you!

- Davis, you demonstrate a "winged energy of delight" that sustains my sense of possibility. Your musicianship is not limited to the piano. You are "playing" your young life beautifully. Tu es adorable!

And thank you to Theresa – the inimitable "T-Rex" – in whom, 20 years on, I find a generosity and devotion that I never imagined possible. You are strong and lovely, fiery and funny. A true partner.

Finally, here's to Rule Number Six. A simpler way to a saner world.

This is not the end of a book; it's another step in a more daring life.

What's next?

SOURCES

William Stafford, "A Course in Creative Writing," *The Way It Is: New and Selected Poems.* Copyright © 1982, 1998 by William Stafford and the Estate of William Stafford. Used with the permission of The Permissions Company, Inc. on behalf of Graywolf Press, Minneapolis, Minnesota, www.graywolfpress.org.

PREFACE

Mary Oliver, "The Journey," *Dream Work* (New York: Atlantic Monthly Press, 1986).

Walt Whitman, "O Me! O Life!" *Leaves of Grass* (1892).

Dead Poets Society, directed by Peter Weir; produced by Steven Haft, Duncan Henderson, Paul Junger Witt, and Tony Thomas. Copyright © 1989 Touchstone Pictures.

Cheryl Strayed, *Tiny Beautiful Things: Advice on Love and Life from Dear Sugar* (New York: Vintage, 2012).

John Updike, *Self-Consciousness: Memoirs* (New York: Fawcett, 1990).

Confucius:
http://www.goodreads.com/quotes/876147-words-are-the-voice-of-the-heart.

John F. Kennedy quote: from a speech prepared for delivery in Dallas the day of his assassination, November 22, 1963.
http://www.quotationspage.com/quote/3225.html.

PART ONE: THE VOICE OF UNDERSTANDING

Introduction
Flannery O'Connor, *Mystery and Manners: Occasional Prose* (New York: Farrar, Straus & Giroux, 1969).

My Dragon Tail
Doug Silsbee, *Presence-Based Leadership Development*, http://www.presencebasedcoaching.com/doug/tail.

The Fire Forest
R. Todd Engstrom, et al., *The Natural History of the Fire Forest*, http://sherpaguides.com/georgia/fire_forest/natural_history.

Small Things: A Winter Essay
Andy Goldsworthy, *Time* (New York: Harry N. Abrams, Inc., 2008).

Getting Ready: A Spring Essay
Pamela McLean, *The Completely Revised Handbook of Coaching: A Developmental Approach* (San Francisco: Jossey-Bass, 2012)

Who Am I Being?
Benjamin Zander, "The Transformative Power of Classical Music," *Ted Talks*, filmed February 2008.

Every Good Boy Does Fine
Jeremy Denk, "Every Good Boy Does Fine," *New Yorker*, April 8, 2013). http://www.newyorker.com/magazine/2013/04/08/every-good-boy-does-fine

How to Be Invisible
Truman Capote, *Other Voices, Other Rooms* (New York: Random House, 1948).

Steven Pressfield, *The War of Art: Break Through the Blocks and Win Your Inner Creative Battles* (New York: Rugged Land, 2002).

Original
Raiders of the Lost Ark, directed by Steven Spielberg; produced by Howard Kazanjian, George Lucas, et al. Copyright © 1981 Paramount Pictures.

Jean-Léon Gérôme (1824-1904). *Pygmalion and Galatea* (ca. 1890). Oil on canvas. 88.9 x 68.6 cm. Metropolitan Museum of Art/Art Resource, New York.

Start Within
Louis CK, interviewed by Conan O'Brien, *Late Night with Conan O'Brien*, Turner Broadcasting System, September 19, 2013.

Stop
Anne Lamott, *Traveling Mercies: Some Thoughts on Faith* (New York: Pantheon, 1999).

Grown Up
Sandra Cisneros, "Eleven," *Woman Hollering Creek and Other Stories* (New York: Random House, 1991).

Inevitable
Matt Linderman, "Robert Rauschenberg on Process, Change, Boredom and More," *Signal v. Noise*, May 16, 2008. https://signalvnoise.com/posts/1029-robert-rauschenberg-on-process-change-boredom-and-more

Wonder
Saint Augustine, *The Confessions* (New York: Vintage, 1998).

Reflective
Krista Tippett, interview with Parker Palmer, "Repossessing Virtue: Economic Crisis, Morality, and Meaning," *On Being*, July 23, 2009 broadcast.

A Model Manager
Tyler Kepner, "Four Days That Inspired Torre's Four Rings," *New York Times*, August 21, 2014).
http://www.nytimes.com/2014/08/22/sports/baseball/amid-his-4-rings-its-joe-torres-own-story-that-stands-out.html?_r=1.

Here
"Proverbs and Song: Verse XXIX" from *Times Alone: Selected Poems of Antonio Machado* translated by Robert Bly © 1983 by Antonio Machado. Reprinted with permission of Wesleyan University Press, www.wesleyan.edu/wespress.

The Door of Integrity
Wendell Berry, *What Are People For* (San Francisco: North Point Press,1990).

Viktor Frankl, *Man's Search for Meaning* (Boston: Beacon Press, 2006 [1946]).

Who You Are
Karen Horney, *Our Inner Conflicts: A Constructive Theory of Neurosis* (New York: Norton, 1945).

PART TWO: THE VOICE OF CONNECTION

Introduction

David Whyte, "Everything Is Waiting for You," *River Flow: New and Selected Poems*, © Many Rivers Press, Langley, WA. Reprinted with permission from Many Rivers Press, www.davidwhyte.com.

George Bernard Shaw, http://www.quotes.net/quote/34524.

Harry Stack Sullivan, *The Interpersonal Theory of Psychiatry* (New York: Tavistock Press, 1953).

Team Spirit

Peter M. Senge, *The Fifth Discipline: The Art & Practice of the Learning Organization* (New York: Currency, 1990).

Bubblegum, RIP

Shrek, directed by Andrew Adamson and Vicky Jensen; produced by Ted Elliott, Penney Finkelman Cox, et al. Copyright © 2001 Dreamworks.

Graduation Day

The Incredibles, directed by Brad Bird; produced by John Lasseter, Kori Rae, Katherine Sarafian and John Walker. Copyright © 2004 Walt Disney Pictures.

All My Fears and Failures

Hillsong United, "Mighty to Save," *The I Heart Revolution: With Hearts as One* (Australia: Hillsong Music, 2008).

I Am The Kind Of Person Who...

For an overview of the Johari Window, see http://www.usc.edu/hsc/ebnet/Cc/awareness/Johari%20windowexplain.pdf.

Your Attention

John C. Merriam quote from plaque at the Yavapai Point Trailside Museum on the South Rim of the Grand Canyon. Merriam was the founder of the museum and president of the Carnegie Institution.

How to Build Capability Before You Need It

J.K. Rowling, *Harry Potter and the Sorcerer's Stone* (New York: Scholastic, 1997).

Michael Maccoby, *Narcissistic Leaders: Who Succeeds and Who Fails* (Cambridge, MA: Harvard Business School Press, 2007).

Manfred Kets de Vries, *The Leader on the Couch: A Clinical Approach to Changing People & Organizations* (San Francisco: Jossey-Bass, 2006).

The Messy Human Real Thing
H.L. Mencken, "The Divine Afflatus," *New York Evening Mail* (16 November 1917); later published in *Prejudices: Second Series* (1920) and *A Mencken Chrestomathy* (1949).

Others
Richard Rohr, "Seeing Our Shadow," *Richard Rohr's Daily Meditation*, March 6, 2015. Adapted from *Things Hidden: Scripture as Spirituality*, (Cincinnati, Ohio: St. Anthony Messenger Press, 2008, 76-77).

Always On
Abraham Maslow, "A Theory of Human Motivation," *Psychological Review*, 1943, 50, 4, 370-96.

Good Enough
Jennifer Kunst, "In Search of the Good Enough Mother," *Psychology Today*, May 9, 2012.

Donald W. Winnicott, "Transitional objects and transitional phenomena," *International Journal of Psychoanalysis*, 1953, 34, 89-97.

James Michener, "When Does Education Stop? *Reader's Digest*, 1962.

Abraham Lincoln, "Annual Message to Congress, December 1, 1862." http://www.abrahamlincolnonline.org/lincoln/speeches/congress.htm.

Connection: 25 Days
Michael Bierut, "Five Years of 100 Days," *Design Observer Group*, February 10, 2011. http://designobserver.com/feature/five-years-of-100-days/24678.

Connection: 50 Days
José Ortega y Gassett, *Man and Crisis* (New York: Norton, 1962).

Small Moves: 100 Days of Connection
G. W. F. Hegel quote http://www.academia.edu/1727742/_What_is_Familiar_is_not_Understood_Precisely_Because_it_is_Familiar_._A_Re-Examination_of_McDowell_s_Quietism_

Contact, directed by Robert Zemeckis; produced by Joan Bradshaw, Lynda Obst, Ann Druyan, Steven Boyd, et al. Copyright © 1997 Warner Brothers.

PART THREE: THE VOICE OF EXPLORATION

Introduction

e.e.cummings quote, http://thinkexist.com/quotation/once_we_believe_in_ourselves-we_can_risk/147522.html.

Exploring the Edge

Dewitt Jones, *Celebrate What's Right with the World* (St. Paul, MN: Star Thrower Distribution, 2013).

Meeting Henry

Seth Godin, *Linchpin: Are You Indispensable?* (New York: Portfolio, 2010).

Labor Day

Judith Michaelson, "Chagall, Artist of Joy and Suffering, Dies," *Los Angeles Times*, March 29, 1985.

James Michener, "When Does Education Stop?" *Reader's Digest*, 1962.

David Whyte, *The Heart Aroused: Poetry and the Preservation of the Soul in Corporate America* (New York: Doubleday, 1994).

Albert Camus, http://voiceseducation.org/content/albert-camus.

Hope, Faith, Love

Reinhold Niebuhr, *The Irony of American History* (Chicago: University of Chicago Press, 2008).

Through the Eye of the Needle

Willy Wonka and the Chocolate Factory, directed by Mel Stuart; produced by Stan Margulies and David Wolper. Copyright © 1971 Paramount Pictures.

Stranger In a Strange Land

"Proverbs and Song: Verse XXIX" from *Times Alone: Selected Poems of Antonio Machado* translated by Robert Bly © 1983 by Antonio Machado. Reprinted with permission of Wesleyan University Press, www.wesleyan.edu/wespress.

Rules for Art Repurposed

Description of risk takers from "The IB Learner Profile," International Baccalaureate Organization, 2013.

Telephone poles, Fence Posts, Railroad Ties

Ira Glass, "Hit the Road," *This American Life* (Episode 494, May 3, 2013).

Learning Starts with Yes (updated)
George Lucas quote: http://www.azquotes.com/quote/811753.

When In Doubt, Shut Up and Listen
Photo credit: Dennis Baggett

Walking
Søren Kierkegaard quote: http://www.goodreads.com/quotes/76117-i-have-walked-myself-into-my-best-thoughts-and-i.

On the Edge of the Inside
Richard Rohr, "A Self-Balancing System," *Richard Rohr's Daily Meditation*, February 18, 2015.

If Only
Rosamund Stone Zander & Benjamin Zander, *The Art of Possibility: Transforming Professional and Personal Life* (Boston: Harvard Business School Press, 2000).

Room to Run
David Whyte, "Out On the Ocean," *River Flow: New and Selected Poems*, © Many Rivers Press, Langley, WA USA. Reprinted with permission from Many Rivers Press, www.davidwhyte.com.

AFTERWORD

Terry Tempest Williams, *When Women Were Birds: Fifty-four Variations on Voice* (New York: Picador, 2013).

ACKNOWLEDGEMENTS

Ralph Waldo Emerson quote: http://www.goodreads.com/quotes/74783-what-i-need-is-someone-who-will-make-me-do.

Rainer Maria Rilke, *The Selected Poetry of Rainer Maria Rilke*, translated by Stephen Mitchell (New York: Vintage, 1989).

Rule Number Six is from: Rosamund Stone Zander & Benjamin Zander, *The Art of Possibility: Transforming Professional and Personal Life* (Boston: Harvard Business School Press, 2000).

All photos by David Berry unless otherwise indicated.

A note on the title:

In November 2010 I attended a one-day launch event for the Institute for Conversational Leadership at the Whidbey Institute near Seattle, Washington. Early in the day one of the other participants shared a story of how her mother or grandmother (I cannot recall which) used to ask this question of her family: Are we not safer leading a more daring life? The question had both immediate and deep resonance for me, as I have attempted to convey in these pages. I have tried to locate the person who shared this anecdote both for the purpose of asking permission and to give appropriate credit but I have been unsuccessful in doing so. I decided to proceed with the use of a portion of the phrase in my title and I am hopeful that by doing so it may come to the attention of the individual who shared it or a member of her family. I look forward to providing full and appropriate credit if and when I am able to do so.

Made in the USA
San Bernardino, CA
09 June 2016